Supporting Care Practice

Level

2

Foundation Modern Apprenticeship

Yvonne Nolan

www.heinemann.co.uk
✓ Free online support
✓ Useful weblinks
✓ 24 hour online ordering

01865 888058

Heinemann Educational Publishers
Halley Court, Jordan Hill, Oxford OX2 8EJ
Part of Harcourt Education

Heinemann is the registered trademark of
Harcourt Education Limited

© Yvonne Nolan, 2004

First published 2004

09 08 07 06 05 04
10 9 8 7 6 5 4 3 2 1

British Library Cataloguing in Publication Data is available
from the British Library on request.

ISBN 0 435 40141 6

Edited by Jan Doorly
Designed by Artistix
Typeset and illustrated by Techtype, Abingdon

Original illustrations © Harcourt Education Limited, 2004

Cover design by Wooden Ark
Printed by The Bath Press Ltd
Cover photo: © Getty

Contents

Acknowledgements

Every effort has been made to contact copyright holders of material reproduced in this book. Any omissions will be rectified in subsequent printings if notice is given to the publishers.

The authors and publishers would like to thank the following for permission to reproduce photographs.

Alamy: page 135
John Birdsall Photography: page 12
Harcourt Education Ltd/Gareth Boden: pages 2, 16, 24, 61, 62, 71, 83, 95, 108, 112, 151
Robert Harding Picture Library: page 131
Science Photo Library: page 58

The author and publishers would like to thank the City and Guilds of London Institute for permission to reproduce sample test questions and glossary. City & Guilds accepts no liability for the contents of this book.

Introduction

Choosing a career in care means that you have opted for one of the most rewarding jobs. You will have the opportunity to enable, empower and support those who use social care and health services. The fact that you have reached the stage of working towards a qualification shows that you have the first, all-important building blocks to develop a successful career in care. The best care professionals realise that caring is about much more than just being a 'kind person' or someone who 'likes people' – those factors are important, but they need to be backed up with a great deal of knowledge and understanding, and a wide range of skills.

As you progress through your Certificate in Supporting Care Practice, you will be developing an understanding of the rights, needs and hopes of the service users you work with. You will also learn about the important skills you need in order to work effectively in care. The Technical Certificate forms part of the Modern Apprenticeship programme in care, so you are likely to be studying this qualification alongside the assessment of your NVQ. This provides you with an excellent chance to learn at the same time as gaining practical skills, and you should have every opportunity to put your knowledge into practice.

The book is designed to match the units in your qualification. Each of the units has several outcomes. These show what you will know by the time you have finished learning all the information in the unit. For example, in Unit 1; when you have completed all the learning in the first outcome, you will be able to:

▶ establish people's rights and how they can be enabled to exercise these.

The sections in this book covering each outcome contain all the knowledge you will need to complete the outcomes. Throughout the book you will find ideas on how your knowledge can be applied in your own workplace, in the form of 'Check it out' activities. Take the time to work through each of these, because you will be surprised at how much more you remember about ideas and knowledge you have tried out in practice.

There are also Case Studies throughout the book, which will provide you with the chance to think about, and discuss with others, some of the situations you may be faced with in doing your job.

At the end of each outcome, you will find an activity that is designed to help you provide evidence for your Key Skills award. The activities are relevant to the outcomes and will help you to think about what you have learned. On page 169 there is a table showing where opportunities for demonstrating Key Skills are provided in these activities.

You will need to complete an assignment set by City and Guilds in order to show that you have successfully achieved the requirements of each unit. There is also a written test which covers knowledge from all of the units in the qualification. Here are some examples of the types of questions you can expect in this test.

---

1 a) State FIVE actions you could take to ensure you support an individual's beliefs and values.

b) Describe briefly FIVE aspects of an individual's life which would be dependent on their values and beliefs.

2 a) Name THREE pieces of legislation that are concerned with people's rights.

b) Outline THREE ways that you could assist your clients in respect of their rights.

3 a) List FOUR actions one could take to establish a positive relationship with a client.

b) Give FOUR differences that exist between a personal and a professional relationship.

4 a) State FIVE factors to support effective communication.

b) Outline FOUR ways of assisting communication with a client who has the following impairments:

i) hearing

ii) visual.

Sample test questions are available from City and Guilds. It is a good idea to practise writing some answers, so that you gain confidence.

On page 167, the Glossary of Terms produced by City and Guilds for this qualification is reproduced. Make sure you understand all these terms before you take your test.

I hope that what you learn from this book will help you to enjoy the work you carry out, and that you will continue to expand and develop your own knowledge and skills throughout your career.

Good luck with your course.
Yvonne Nolan

Equality and the provision of care

This is the essential unit which will underpin all the work you do in a care setting. Regardless of the task you are undertaking, or the service user you are working with, everything you do must be carried out in accordance with the principles you will learn here. By the time you have successfully completed this unit you will know about service users' rights and how to safeguard them. You will also have learned about the important differences between the values and beliefs of individuals, and how these differences contribute to the overall quality and richness of local and national communities. You will know how you can make sure that you recognise and respect difference in the way you practise.

This unit will give you the opportunity to look at your own performance in a care setting and help you to practise in a way which is anti-discriminatory and anti-oppressive. On completing this unit you will understand the importance of confidentiality and how to make sure you comply with legislation and guidelines.

Outcome 1: Establish people's rights and how they can be enabled to exercise these

The rights your service users have

Rights and responsibilities are a huge subject. In order to look at rights in terms of how they affect the people you work with and provide care for, it is helpful to discuss them under the following headings:

▶ basic human rights
▶ rights under charters, guidelines and policies
▶ rights provided by law.

What are responsibilities? They are the other side of the coin to rights – most of our responsibilities are about protecting, improving or not infringing other people's rights. Responsibilities are the balance for rights, and it is impossible to consider one without the other.

Basic human rights

In 1949 the United Nations Universal Declaration of Human Rights identified a set of basic rights which everyone should have. The Declaration sets out to

Everyone has personal rights, but they must be balanced with responsibilities to others.

promote and encourage acceptance of personal, civil, political, economic, social and cultural rights, which are only limited by the need to respect the rights and freedoms of others and the needs of morality, public order and general welfare.

For many people throughout the world, these are rights they can only hope for, and not rights they currently enjoy. The United Nations has a Commission on Human Rights which works to promote the world-wide acceptance of these basic rights and to identify abuses and violations of human rights throughout the world.

Personal basic rights

Alongside the basic rights conferred by charters and laws, there are also personal rights which apply to all of us. For example, someone may say 'I've got a right to be angry, haven't I?' Of course everyone has a right to be angry, or to be upset or frustrated when things go wrong, or to feel vulnerable and afraid in new or threatening situations. Everyone has a right to feel and express basic human emotions, but the responsibility that goes alongside this is that you cannot express them in a way which oppresses or harms someone else.

This is not always an easy area for workers in care settings to manage. A service user who is angry about or frustrated by his or her condition may express some of the anger by being rude or aggressive to other service users. Clearly, this cannot be allowed to happen, because there is always an important balance to be achieved between the rights of the service user and the rights of others.

There are balances in the exercise of other personal rights, such as the right to make mistakes or to get things wrong. Of course everyone is entitled to try out new ideas and to explore and develop as an individual. This inevitably will lead to mistakes and errors. Most of the time this is acknowledged as an essential part of the learning process. As the saying goes, 'the person who never made a mistake never made anything'. However, as always, there are balances to be found. Some people have less room to make mistakes than others:

▶ an air traffic controller who makes a mistake could be the cause of a major catastrophe
▶ a lorry, bus or train driver who makes a mistake could cause disaster on a large scale
▶ a health professional who prescribes or administers the wrong medication could cause major damage.

In general, everyone should be able to make mistakes without being ridiculed or humiliated. But there will always be some exceptional circumstances where mistakes cannot be tolerated.

Rights under charters, guidelines and policies

These are rights which do not have the force of law, but which are designed to improve the services people receive.

The document called 'Your Guide to the NHS', published in 2000, sets out what people can expect from the National Health Service. It covers issues such as people's rights to receive care from a GP, how long they can reasonably be expected to wait for a hospital appointment, and how long before urgent and non-urgent treatment. However, it is different from the Patient's Charter which it replaced because it also identifies the responsibilities of patients (see page 14). The guide includes information on how patients can use services and how they can complain if necessary.

Even though this is set out as only a guidance document, the government has made it clear that this is the way in which the Health Service is expected to operate. This means that the performance of all NHS trusts is measured against this guidance.

Charters exist for other services, such as the Passenger's Charter, which lays down standards which can be expected for rail travel.

The key role of charters is to make the expected standards public, so there can be no argument that service users are being unreasonable in their demands, or their expectations are too high. If people know what they have a right to expect, then they can take steps to complain and have things put right if the standards are not met.

Rights provided by law

The Human Rights Act received the royal assent on 9 November 1998 and the majority of its provisions came into force on 2 October 2000. The Human Rights Act means that residents of the United Kingdom – this Act applies in England, Scotland, Wales and Northern Ireland – will now be entitled to seek help from the courts if they believe that their human rights have been infringed.

Organisations subject to the Human Rights Act 1998

Residential homes or nursing homes	These perform functions which would otherwise be performed by a local authority
Charities	
Voluntary organisations	
Public service	This could include the privatised utilities, such as gas, electric and water companies

It is likely that anyone who works in health or care will be working within the provisions of the Human Rights Act, which guarantees the following rights.

1 **The right to life.** Public authorities must not cause the death of any person and they have a positive duty to protect life.

2 **The right to freedom from torture and inhuman or degrading treatment or punishment.** This ill-treatment relates to both mental and physical suffering. One of the factors which is taken into account under this right is the severity and duration of the torture, inhuman or degrading treatment and the vulnerability of the victim.

3 **The right to freedom from slavery, servitude and forced or compulsory labour.** Slavery means that a person is owned by somebody else like a piece of property. Servitude is defined as a person not being owned by someone else but being forced to provide service for them and unable to leave.

4 **The right to liberty and security of person.** People have a right not to be arrested or detained except when the detention is authorised by law.

5 **The right to a fair and a public trial within a reasonable time.** This right covers all criminal and most civil cases as well as tribunals and some internal hearings.

6 **The right to freedom from retrospective criminal law and no punishment without law.** This right means that people cannot be convicted for an act which was not a criminal offence at the time it was committed, nor can they face a punishment which was not in force when the act happened.

7 **The right to respect for private and family life, home and correspondence.** This is one of the very far-reaching parts of the Human Rights Act. Public authorities may only interfere in someone's private life when they have the legal authority to do so.

8   **The right to freedom of thought, conscience and religion.** Under this right people can hold whatever thoughts, positions of conscience or religious beliefs they wish.

9   **The right to freedom of expression.** Freedom of expression includes what is said in conversation or speeches, what is published in books, articles or leaflets, what is broadcast and what is presented as art or placed on the Internet. In fact, any means of communication.

10 **The right to freedom of assembly and association.** This includes the right of people to demonstrate peacefully and to join or choose not to join trade unions.

11 **The right to marry and found a family.** This part of the Act is particularly relevant to rules and policies concerning adoption and fostering.

12 **The prohibition of discrimination in the enjoyment of convention rights.** The Act recognises that not all differences in treatment are discriminatory; those that are discriminating are defined as those which have no objective or reasonable justification.

13 **The right to peaceful enjoyment of possessions and protection of property.** The Act defines many possessions as property; not just houses or cars, but things like shares, licences and goodwill.

14 **The right of access to an education.** The right of access to education must be balanced against the resources available. This right may be relevant to the exclusion of disruptive pupils from schools, and may also prove to be very relevant for children with special needs.

15 **The right of free elections.** They must be free and fair and be held at reasonable intervals. Access issues are also involved, such as making sure that people with disabilities or those who are ill are still able to participate.

16 **The right not to be subjected to the death penalty.** This provision abolishes the death penalty.

Law, rights and discrimination

Discrimination is a denial of rights. Discrimination can be based on race, gender, disability or sexual orientation. The main Acts of Parliament which are to do with rights are:

▶ the Race Relations Act 1976
▶ the Equal Pay Act 1970
▶ the Sex Discrimination Act 1975
▶ the Disability Discrimination Act 1995.

Race Relations Act 1976

This Act prohibits all forms of racial discrimination, whether in employment, housing or services. It also makes it an offence to incite (encourage) racial hatred. The Act covers all discrimination whether it is about colour, nationality or race, and forbids both direct and indirect discrimination.

Direct discrimination occurs when someone is stopped from doing something because of their race as, for example, in the two adverts shown on the next page.

> **English workers wanted for new factory**
> **Good wages**

> **Flat to let**
> **Two bedrooms**
> **No Irish applicants please**

Both of those adverts are blatantly racist and would not be seen anywhere today, but 50 years ago such adverts were commonplace.

Indirect discrimination is more subtle. This can work by imposing conditions which some people would find impossible to meet, as in the advert below, for example.

> **Bricklayer required**
> **Must speak fluent English**

This is indirect discrimination because it may exclude people who are fairly recent immigrants. There can be no justification for this requirement if the work does not require use of language or contact with the public.

Another example might be a sheltered housing scheme which has a rule about tenants not being allowed to cook highly spiced food because of the smell. It would be breaking the law, because Asian food tends to be highly spiced whereas English food does not. This would discriminate against Asian tenants being able to cook their native food.

People's rights to housing and provision of services are also supported by the Act.

Sounds great …

but – *the rights can be difficult to enforce. Support is given to people bringing cases under the Act by the Commission for Racial Equality, but proving discrimination is notoriously difficult.*

DID YOU KNOW?

Women comprise 50 per cent of the world population, do 90 per cent of the world's work, earn 10 per cent of the world's income and own 1 per cent of the world's wealth. (UNESCO)

The Equal Pay Act 1970

The Equal Pay Act 1970 (amended 1983) is designed to make discrimination on the grounds of gender illegal. It provides a woman with the right to be employed on the same terms and conditions as a man doing an equivalent job, or work of equal value. For example, it has been judged in a court of law that a female canteen cook's work is of equal value to that of a male joiner, painter or sanitation engineer.

This type of legislation is common in many countries now, so the situation for women's pay has improved.

Sounds great …

but – *it is often the kind of work which women do, much of it part-time or low-paid, which causes the difference in average pay*

but – *of course, the work which women do at home is unpaid!*

DID YOU KNOW?

Average male wages in the UK are still about one-third higher than women's. In the past 30 years that figure has improved by only around 17 per cent. In 1965, women's average wage was half that of men.

Sex Discrimination Act 1975

This Act is designed to provide equal rights to men and women in respect of employment, goods, services and facilities. It prevents discrimination either directly or indirectly which would prevent women from being employed or receiving a service in the same way as men. The Equal Opportunities Commission supports the working of the law by supporting cases, investigating abuses and promoting equality.

Women who, for example, have been repeatedly passed over for promotion at work, even though men who are less qualified have achieved success, can use the Sex Discrimination Act. There have been several well-publicised cases in public services like the police and fire services.

Women have a right to be admitted to all public places on the same basis as men. This means that there are no longer any 'men only' bars – unless they are in private clubs, such as golf clubs.

Men can also use the Act if they have been unfairly discriminated against. For example, the fact that most baby-changing facilities are located in women's public lavatories means that a man who has the care of a baby will have difficulty finding a suitable place to change the baby.

The Act deals with both direct and indirect discrimination. For example, a woman could take an employer to court if a job was advertised like the one below.

> ## Care assistants needed for residential home
> Must be experienced. Applicants should be at least 5 ft 10 in tall.

Height is not a reasonable requirement in order to do the job. Far more women are below 5ft 10in than men, so the advert discriminates against women.

It would also be discriminatory against men if it advertised for people under 5ft 4in!

In the provision of services, if, for instance, a primary care team decided no longer to provide treatment for people with osteoporosis, a challenge could be made on the grounds that it is primarily women who suffer from the condition and therefore the decision would discriminate unfairly against women. Similarly, if the group decided not to treat people with prostate problems, the decision could be open to challenge by men.

Sounds great …

but – *like racial discrimination, sex discrimination is difficult to prove.*

CASE STUDY

The A family live in the Midlands. Mr A is from Pakistan, and he is very devout in his Muslim beliefs. The tradition in the area he comes from is that all young men and women are expected to have their marriages arranged by their families. Mr A's daughter M is 16 years old, and she was born in the UK, speaks with a local accent, and has friends, both Muslim and non-Muslim, in the area. However, her father has now decided that it is time she was married. He has arranged for her to be married to a distant relative from the family's home town in Pakistan. M is not happy at the prospect, and wants to meet someone in the UK. She is reluctant to go to Pakistan, where she has never been before.

1 What are Mr A's rights? What are his responsibilities?
2 What are M's rights?
3 Does M have responsibilities?
4 What decisions could be made?
5 Do any laws affect this situation?

Disability Discrimination Act 1995

This Act is designed to provide rights for people with disabilities in:

▶ employment
▶ access to education and transport
▶ housing
▶ obtaining goods and services.

The Act defines disability as a condition which makes it difficult for someone to carry out normal day-to-day activities. The disability can be physical, sensory (affecting the senses) or mental but, to be covered by the Act, it must be substantial and have a long-term effect. This means that the disability must last, or be expected to last, for at least 12 months.

Under the Act employers must not treat a disabled person less favourably than an able-bodied person. An employer must examine the changes that need to be made to the workplace, or to how the work is carried out, in order to make it possible for someone with a disability to do the job.

Access rights to education and transport for people with disabilities means that schools and colleges have to produce details of how any student will be able to access courses, regardless of disability. All new taxis, buses, trains and coaches have to be accessible for disabled people.

Landlords are not allowed to discriminate against anyone with a disability when letting a property, or to charge a higher rent than they would for a non-disabled person.

Shops, restaurants and anyone who provides a service have to ensure that disabled people are able to make use of the service and are not charged more than a non-disabled person. They have to make it easier for disabled people to use their services by providing any adaptations needed or by arranging for other ways of using the service, for example by providing a mail order catalogue.

Sounds great …

but – *most of the provisions are only enforced 'if it is reasonable to do so'*

but – *one of the considerations which people can take into account when considering if it is 'reasonable' to change things for disabled people is the cost – so, if it would cost too much to put in a ramp, the shop can justify not doing so.*

DID YOU KNOW?

There are over 6.5 million disabled people in the UK – and 31 per cent of these are currently employed.

Only 17 per cent of disabled people were born with their disability.

REMEMBER

▶ Acts of Parliament don't change attitudes.

▶ Discrimination may be unlawful, but people still have the right to think, write and speak as they wish.

Particular laws for particular people

Apart from the laws which provide rights for everyone, there are other laws which are likely to affect the particular group of individuals you work with. These laws are not only about providing people with rights, they can also be about restricting rights, when it is in someone's interests to do so.

Mental Health Act 1983

This Act affects people with mental health problems or a learning disability. People can be compulsorily sent to hospital when they are considered to be ill, or to prison if they have committed criminal offences. This is a severe restriction on people's liberty and they have rights to appeal against such detentions. Appeals are heard by special tribunals, and it is easy to see the dilemma which could exist between the rights of an individual and responsibility towards the community.

CASE STUDY

K was convicted 10 years ago of sexually abusing two children. He was diagnosed as suffering from a mental illness, and so was committed to a secure hospital under the Mental Health Act rather than being sent to prison. This type of sentence does not carry a particular length of time, but is referred to as HMP (at Her Majesty's pleasure). This means that the person will remain in a special hospital until enough evidence is put before a tribunal for a decision to be made that he or she no longer represents a risk.

K is now in his late fifties and all the psychiatric specialists are of the opinion that his illness is now 'burnt out' and he does not represent a threat to the community. His future is about to be considered by a tribunal who have the power to allow him to be released. K is a pleasant man, who is very 'slow' in his responses. He is not at all aggressive and is very eager to please. He will do exactly as instructed, and has spent the past three years helping in the hospital kitchens. He cannot cope with complicated tasks, but can do simple jobs which do not involve much memory.

However, the local community where he lived and assaulted the children has heard about the possibility of release. There is a great deal of concern, and a local campaign has begun which claims that the tribunal has a responsibility to consider the safety of the local community. There have been threats that K will be the subject of a vigilante campaign if he is released, and the implication is that he may be harmed or forced to leave the area.

1 Whose rights should be considered in this situation?
2 Is there a responsibility for the tribunal and the psychiatrists to consider the community?
3 Whose rights are most important?
4 How could this be resolved?

The Children Act 1989

This Act provides children with the right to be protected from 'significant harm'. The definition of significant harm is decided by the courts at the request of social services departments. The harm could be being inflicted by parents, or by the children themselves if they are 'beyond control' and involved in crime, drugs or prostitution.

This is also the first Act which identifies 'parental responsibility' rather than 'parental rights'. So, for the first time, children are not treated as property over which 'rights' can be exercised.

This Act also ensures that nurseries and residential schools have to reach certain standards, and that they are regularly inspected.

It gives rights to children who have been looked after by social services departments to be supported, to be assisted to become independent, and to have access to information about their lives and their own histories.

CASE STUDY

C is 15 years old. She is at a police station refusing to return home. She says that she does not get on with her parents because they are too strict and do not give her any freedom. C wants to be able to go to clubs and go out with boys, which her parents will not allow. She says that she would rather live in a children's home because there she will be allowed more freedom. She is friendly with K, a girl at her school who lives in a small children's home. C feels that K goes out and has boyfriends and can do more or less what she likes. She says that if the police or social workers send her home to her parents, then she will run away. Her parents want her to return home, and her father has arrived at the police station insisting that he is taking her home.

1 What rights does C have?
2 What rights do her parents have?
3 Do social services have any responsibility for C's safety?
4 How can this be resolved?

NHS and Community Care Act 1990

This Act gives older and disabled people rights in respect of the services they should be provided with by their social services department.

All social services departments have to publish plans about how they will run their services. These plans must include the criteria which will be used to define how services will be provided for particular needs. Everyone has a right to see the plans, and to be consulted if they belong to a group which represents people who are likely to use the services.

All people who are in need of community care have the legal right to have their needs assessed and to have services provided.

All people who are in need of community care have the right to have their needs assessed and to have services provided in accordance with the published standards. People also have a right to complain if the service is not provided.

This is a wide-ranging Act which has provided disabled and older people with more rights than they previously enjoyed, although many social services departments are struggling to provide the services with a limited amount of funding.

CASE STUDY

Mrs B is 93 years old. She cannot get out of bed, has a heart condition, emphysema and severe arthritis and requires round-the-clock care. She is unable to care for herself at all; she is unable to get out of bed without help and is extremely frail. If she were left alone she would be in grave danger of falling or she might need help with using her oxygen supply. Mrs B is not in the slightest bit confused and is very clear that she does not wish to leave her home and go into residential or nursing home care. The local NHS trust will not keep her in hospital as she does not have any acute medical needs that cannot be met in the community.

Her needs assessment has defined that she needs 24-hour care. This is presently provided by a team of carers who work for a local private care agency. The cost is several times more than the cost of providing the equivalent care in a residential setting. The local social services department is presently having to refuse services to some people because of a shortage of cash. This has been explained to Mrs B in an attempt to persuade her to agree to residential care, but she continues to insist that she wants to remain in her own home.

1 Does Mrs B have the right to insist on staying at home?
2 What are the responsibilities of social services to Mrs B? And to others in need?
3 Should Mrs B's rights be more important than the responsibilities to the rest of the community?

How to balance rights and responsibilities

It is often difficult for people to exercise their rights while ensuring that others' rights are respected. A person may have the right to live as he or she wishes, but what about the rest of the community?

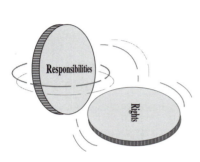

CASE STUDY

G is 53 years old. She has lived alone in a large house since her mother died 10 years ago. She behaves in a strange way, often walking along the road and talking to herself. She does not acknowledge any of the neighbours, apart from shouting at local children if they venture into her very overgrown garden. She appears very dirty and dresses in the same clothes for months on end. G seems to collect old newspapers and her house is crammed with rubbish. She has 18 cats, five dogs, several ducks, 10 chickens and a goat. All the animals are well fed and cared for, but they create a considerable amount of noise and smell.

G has been assessed by a psychiatrist and is not mentally ill. The people in the local community want her to leave. They say that she causes problems with the animals, that the house is a health hazard, she frightens the children and her house is so dilapidated it makes the whole road look scruffy.

1 What rights does G have?
2 What rights do the rest of the community have?
3 Does G have any responsibility to the community she lives in?
4 Do they have any responsibility towards her?
5 How could this be resolved?

Responsibilities

'Responsibility' is a word which has meanings at many levels – it is often used to refer to the duties people take on as they grow up: buying a house, getting married, having children. All of these things bring responsibilities, but it could be argued that these responsibilities conflict with rights.

For example, looking after children is a great responsibility. It also means that people no longer have the right to please themselves about going out, or spending money as they please, because their responsibilities towards their children come before their rights to satisfy their own desires. Most people accept this willingly and take delight in providing care for their children, but some situations are not so clear cut.

Check it out

Does a person's responsibility to care for an elderly parent outweigh his or her rights to earn a living and have a social life? Discuss this with your colleagues.

The National Health Service clearly identifies the responsibilities of patients. While people have a right to expect a certain level of service from the NHS, it is clear that the health of the nation is a two-way partnership and that everyone has a responsibility to contribute. Patient responsibilities were identified in 'Your Guide to the NHS' (2000) as the following:

▶ Do what you can to look after your own health, and follow advice on a healthy lifestyle.
▶ Care for yourself when appropriate. (For example, you can treat yourself at home for common ailments such as coughs, colds and sore throats.)
▶ Give blood if you are able, and carry an organ donor card or special needs card or bracelet.
▶ Keep your appointment or let the GP, dentist, clinic or hospital know as soon as possible if you cannot make it. Book routine appointments in plenty of time.
▶ Listen carefully to advice on your treatment and medication. Tell the doctor about any treatments you are already taking.
▶ Return any equipment that is no longer needed.
▶ Pay NHS prescription charges and any other charges promptly when they are due and claim financial benefits or exemptions from these charges correctly. Treat NHS staff, fellow patients, carers and visitors politely, and with respect. Violence and racial, sexual or verbal harassment are unacceptable.

The dilemma of balancing rights and responsibilities is one most people working in care deal with on a daily basis. Think about your right to go home! There is a set time at which you should finish your shift or your day, but there are many occasions when it is not that simple. An emergency may have arisen, perhaps someone has fallen, or there may have been a death, or someone has just started to talk to you for the first time. You could be dealing with a relative who is very distressed. Any of these situations, and many more, can mean that you balance your right to finish work on time against the responsibilities you hold towards the individual needing your help, and his or her right to be helped.

Constraints and conflicts

Most care settings, whether residential or providing day-care services, involve living, sharing and working with others. Any situation which involves close and prolonged contact with others has the potential to be difficult. You only have to think about the day-to-day conflicts and difficulties which arise in most families to realise the issues involved when human beings get together in a group.

Disagreements between service users, particularly in residential or day-care settings, are not unusual and you may well find yourself being called on to act as referee. The conflicts can range from disputes over particular chairs or TV channels, to political disagreements or complaints about the behaviour of others. Conflict resolution is not an easy task, wherever you are and however large or small a scale you are working on. However, there are some basic guidelines to follow:

▶ remain calm and speak in a firm, quiet voice – do not raise your voice
▶ make it clear that physical violence is completely unacceptable
▶ make it clear that verbal abuse will not be tolerated
▶ listen in turn to both sides of the argument – don't let people interrupt each other
▶ look for reasonable compromises which involve both parties in winning some points and losing others
▶ make it clear to both sides that they will have to compromise – that total victory for one or the other is not an option.

A wide range of difficulties can arise. They can be about behaviour which is unacceptable and causes distress to others, such as playing loud music or shouting. They can also be about matters which seem trivial but can cause major irritation when people live together, such as the way someone eats, or the fact that they mutter out loud as they read the newspaper.

Sometimes conflicts can arise about behaviour which is not anyone's fault, but is the result of someone's illness or condition. For instance, sometimes people experiencing some forms of dementia may shout and moan loudly, which may be distressing and annoying to others. Some people may eat messily or dribble as the result of a physical condition, which may be unpleasant and upsetting for those who share a table with them. These situations require a great deal of tact and explanation. It is simply not possible for the individuals concerned to stop their behaviour, so those around them have to be helped to understand the reasons and to cope with the consequences.

Think about the type of arguments and disagreements which may arise in your work setting. If you have been involved in helping to resolve any such problem, make a note of what you did and how effective it was. If another member of staff was involved, note down the actions he or she took and if they were effective. See if you can work out why some actions were effective. If they were not, see if you can work out why they failed.

Working with colleagues

In any care setting, it is not only the service users who have to be together for long periods of time – the staff have to learn to work together too. This may be

the first time you have worked in a team with colleagues, or you may have moved to a new team which will function differently from the last place you worked. Each team is different!

Teams take time to learn to work together well. They go through various stages as they settle down, and every time a new team member arrives, things change. Not everyone will share the same views about how tasks should be undertaken and about the right course of action on every occasion. Much will depend on how well the team is managed. However, there are some ground rules that can be applied in most situations.

Teams have to learn to get along and work well together.

▶ Find out the ways in which decisions are reached and the team members who should be included.
▶ Always ask for advice and clarify anything you are not sure about.
▶ Do not assume that everything is the same in every workplace.
▶ Recognise that every team member, regardless of his or her role and status, has an essential contribution to make.
▶ Value the input of all colleagues and recognise its importance.
▶ Make sure that the way you work is not increasing the workload of others or hindering them in carrying out their work.

Most workplaces have a means of decision making. There could be planning and review meetings where decisions are made about service provision. Staff meetings may be the forum for making decisions about general practice matters, or there may be specific staff development and training meetings for sharing best practice. Organised meetings run by a line manager or supervisor are the best place for discussing differences about practice or decisions about a particular service user; here everyone has the chance to have a say and to take account of a range of views from other team members. A well-run staff group should also be able to reach agreement on the best course of action and make sure that all the relevant views are taken into account.

Take an example where there is a disagreement between staff members about the extent to which a service user is able to undertake his or her own care. One member of staff may see that it is important to protect the service user from risk, while another feels that the service user's independence should be encouraged. It is essential that both these views are acknowledged as being equally valid and important, and that a compromise is reached which will leave both workers feeling that they have made a contribution to the final actions agreed.

How to support service users in the exercise of their rights

One of the most useful and important things you can do for someone is to give them information. Knowledge is power, and giving someone information empowers them. Working as a carer means that you are often going to be working with people who are vulnerable and who have no confidence or power. You will be able to support them very effectively by helping them to stand up for their rights. Many people you work with will be unaware of the information they need, because:

- ▶ they are unaware that the information exists
- ▶ they do not know how to find it
- ▶ there are physical barriers to accessing information
- ▶ there are emotional barriers to seeking information.

DID YOU KNOW?

Age Concern receives around 16,000 requests for information in a six-month period. When the figures were last analysed, around 25 per cent of the queries were found to be about health and social care, only slightly less about consumer issues (including wills), 10 per cent about financing residential care, and about 20 per cent respectively about income and housing.

If you are going to provide people with information, there are certain basic rules you must observe. There is no point in providing information which is out of date or inaccurate, or in giving people the right information at the wrong time.

Keys to good practice

✔ Make sure that your information is up to date. You may have to contact quite a few places to make sure you have the most accurate information possible. Check the dates on any leaflets you have and contact the producer of the leaflet to see whether it has been replaced.

✔ Go to the most direct source, wherever possible. For example, for information about benefits, contact the Benefits Agency. If you need to know about community care services, contact social services.

✔ Advice services such as the Citizens Advice Bureau are excellent and provide a wide range of information. Make use also of the specialist organisations which represent specific groups, such as Age Concern or Scope.

✔ Check whether the information you are providing has local, regional and national elements. For instance, if you are providing information about Age Concern's services for older people, it is important to provide the local contact as well as national contact points.

✔ The information you provide must be in a format that can be used by the person it is intended for. For example, there is little value in providing an ordinary leaflet to an individual with impaired vision. You will need to obtain large print, taped or braille versions depending on the way in which the individual prefers to receive information.

✔ Consider the language used and provide information in a language which the individual can easily understand. Information is of no value if it is misunderstood.

✔ Provide information at an appropriate time when the individual can make use of it. For example, a man who has just had a leg amputated, following an accident, will not be ready to receive information about the latest design in wheelchairs or how to join in sports for disabled people. He may be interested in 12 months' time, but initially he is going to need information about support groups and practical information about how artificial limbs work, and how to manage to use the toilet!

✔ The information you provide must be relevant and useful. For example, if an individual wants to make a complaint to the Benefits Agency, you will need to find out what the complaints procedure is and provide the relevant information and forms to be completed. A general leaflet about the services of the Benefits Agency would not be as helpful.

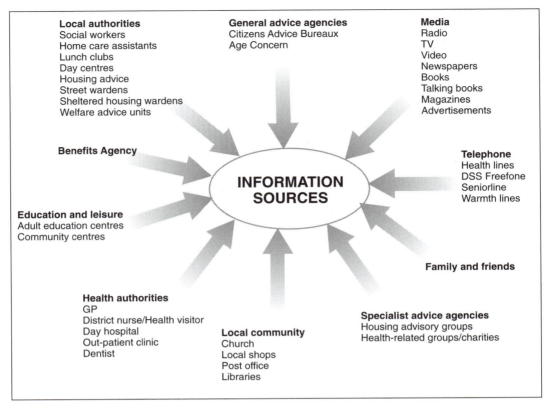

Sources of information.

Helping people who cannot help themselves

There may be occasions when you have identified a person's rights and given him or her the information needed. However, the individual may not be able to exercise those rights effectively. There can be many reasons why people miss out on their rights:

▶ their rights may be infringed by someone else
▶ there may be physical barriers
▶ there may be emotional barriers.

Where people cannot exercise their own rights, it is sometimes important that someone acts on their behalf. If it is within your work role to do so, you could act in a formal or informal way to assist.

Acting to help someone exercise his or her rights in a formal way may involve you speaking on that person's behalf to another agency, for example the Benefits Agency. Before you undertake this role you must check with your manager that it is appropriate for you to do so. Alternatively you may need to contact a professional advocate, such as a welfare rights worker or solicitor, in order to support service users.

You also need to be very sure that you are not assisting someone to exercise his or her rights because you are angered by an injustice. It must be because the individual, possibly based on information you have provided, wants to exercise his or her rights. The key when acting on behalf of another is to consult, and to constantly ensure that you are doing what he or she wishes.

CASE STUDY

Mrs S lives alone on just her state pension. She has never claimed any income support although there is no doubt she would be entitled to it. She struggles to survive on her pension and, by the time she has paid all her bills and fed the cat, there is little left for herself. She eats very little and is reluctant to turn the heating on. Despite being given all the relevant information by her home care assistant, Mrs S will not claim any further benefits. She always says: 'I shall be fine, there are others worse off than me. Let it go to those who need it.'

1 What are Mrs S's rights?
2 Should action be taken on her behalf?
3 Would the situation be different if she had a son with a learning disability who lived with her? Would her rights still be the same? Would her responsibilities still be the same?
4 What would your responsibilities be if you were a carer for Mrs S?

You may also need to defend people's rights in a more informal way during your normal work. For example, people have a right to privacy, and you may need to act to deal with someone who constantly infringes upon that by discussing other people's circumstances in public. You will have to balance the rights of one person against another, and decide whose rights are being infringed. You may decide that a right to privacy is more important than the right to free speech. That may be appropriate in your workplace, but does the same principle apply to politicians and the way they are discussed in the media?

Check it out

An individual's right to rest may be infringed by someone who shouts all night. How would you balance the rights of one person not to be disturbed against the rights of another not to be given medication which is only for the benefit of others?

Complaints

An important part of exercising rights is being able to complain if services are poor or do not meet expectations. All public service organisations are required to have a complaints procedure and to make the procedure readily available for people to use. Part of your role may be to assist service users in making complaints, either directly, by supporting them in following the procedure, or indirectly, by making sure that they are aware of the complaints procedure and are able to follow it.

Complaints to an organisation are an important part of the monitoring process and they should be considered as part of every review of service provision. If all service users simply put up with poor service and no one complains to an organisation, it will never be aware of where the service needs improvement.

The importance of rights

Ensuring that all service users can exercise their rights is an essential part of the role of any worker in a care setting. If you are always conscious of the rights of those you care for, and always aware of the need to make sure those rights are not being infringed or denied, then you cannot fail to deliver a good quality service, and you will be on the road to developing into an excellent practitioner.

Outcome activity 1.1

You can do this activity by yourself, but it is better if you can work in a small group with three or four others.

Choose at least **three** different service users whose rights you will be able to investigate. These may be real service users from your workplace, or they may be relatives or friends. If you cannot find three people for your activity, then you may use up to two imaginary service users.

Make sure that each of the three has at least **one** major difference. This can be:

▶ age
▶ gender
▶ culture
▶ race
▶ level of disability
▶ type of disability
▶ type of service used
▶ any other significant difference.

Ask permission from the service users you are intending to include in your activity. Make sure that you do not identify individual service users during your activity, and explain to the service users that all information about them will remain confidential. You should refer to them by their initials or choose different names. The activity involves the following steps.

Step 1
Research the rights which each of your three service users has. All of them will have the same basic rights which we all have, but there will be some differences because of the significant differences in the service users you have chosen.

You can use a range of ways to find information about rights – the Internet is a useful method of research, along with textbooks. Make a note of all the websites you visit and each of the books you refer to.

Step 2
Discuss in your group, or think about, at least two situations for each service user where he or she would not be able to enjoy the rights you have identified. If you cannot clearly identify two situations for each service user, discuss situations which could result in the service user being unable to exercise his or her rights.

Step 3
Decide in your group, or think about, how the service users can be helped to exercise the rights you have identified. Consider the roles of each of the following:

► the government
► society as a whole
► the organisation providing care
► the individual workers providing care
► relatives and friends.

Step 4
Research and make a list of the responsibilities which balance the rights you have identified. Consider how the exercise of some of the rights may affect other people's rights.

Step 5
Prepare a presentation showing what you have found out about your service users' rights, to be given to your tutor group, or your assessor(s), or a group of colleagues. The presentation can be prepared using handouts, overhead transparencies or using a computer programme such as PowerPoint, depending on the technology available. Plan a discussion after the presentation, using the information you have noted in Step 4.

Step 6
Deliver the presentation and lead the discussion on how to balance responsibilities and rights, and how to help people exercise their rights without infringing the rights of others.

Identify people's different beliefs and values and show how practice encompasses them

What is normal?

The notion of 'normality and abnormality' is very difficult to pin down. What is normal for one person is not for another. For instance, taking off your shoes when entering a holy place is normal for many people, but would be an unusual experience for others. For extended families to share a house is normal in some cultures and definitely not in others. Normality can only ever be 'normal for a specific person' – there is no such thing as 'normal for everyone'. The particular set of circumstances always has to be considered.

Who are you?

Self-esteem is about how we **value** ourselves. Self-concept, or self-image is about how we **see** ourselves. Both are equally important when you are working.

Self-concept is about what makes people who they are. Everyone has a concept of themselves – it can be a positive image overall or a negative one, but a great many factors contribute to an individual sense of identity. These will include:

- ▶ gender
- ▶ race
- ▶ language/accent
- ▶ values and beliefs
- ▶ religion
- ▶ sexual orientation.

All of these are aspects of our lives which contribute to our idea of who we are. As a care worker it is essential that you consider how each of the service users you work with has developed his or her own self-concept and identity, and it is important that you recognise and promote this.

Service users' beliefs

The values, beliefs, tastes and preferences which service users have are what make them who they are. These must be supported, nurtured and encouraged, and not ignored or disregarded because they are inconvenient or don't fit in with the care system.

In your role as a care worker, you will come across situations where a little thought or a small change in practice could make people feel more valued and respected as individuals. For example, you may need to find out how a service user likes to be addressed. Is the use of the title 'Mr' or 'Mrs' considered more respectful and appropriate, or is a first name preferred? This, particularly for some older people, can be one of the ways of indicating respect that is felt to be important.

All service users are different and will have different values and beliefs, including what they prefer to eat

You will need to give thought to the values and beliefs which service users may have, for example:

▶ religious or cultural beliefs about eating certain foods
▶ values concerning forms of dress
▶ beliefs or preferences about who should be able to provide personal care.

What do you need to do?

You need to make sure that people have been asked about religious or cultural preferences and those preferences are recorded so that all care workers and others providing care are able to access them.

There may already be arrangements in your workplace to ask for and record this information. If so, you must ensure that you are familiar with the process and that you know where to find the information for every service user you work with. If your workplace does not have arrangements in place to find out about people's choices and preferences, you should discuss with your line manager ways in which you can help to find this out.

How do you need to do it?

The prospect of having to ask people questions about their background, values and beliefs can be quite daunting. But it is quite rare for people to be offended by your showing an interest in them! Simple, open questions, asked politely, are always the best way: 'Excuse me, Mr Khan, the information I have here notes that you are a Muslim. Can you tell me about any particular foods you do not wish to eat?'

You can obtain some information by observation. For instance, looking at someone can tell you a lot about his or her preferences in dress. Particular forms of clothing worn for religious or cultural reasons are usually obvious (a turban or a sari, for instance, is easy to spot) but other forms of dress may also give you some clues about the person wearing them. Think about how dress can tell you about the amount of money people are used to spending on clothes, or what kind of background they come from. Clothes also tell you a lot about someone's age and the type of lifestyle they are likely to be used to. Beware, however – any information you think you gain from this type of observation must be confirmed by checking your facts. Otherwise it is easy to be caught out – some people from wealthy backgrounds wear cheap clothes, and some people in their seventies wear the latest fashions and have face lifts!

Planning for individuals

The process of providing care should be carefully planned and designed to ensure that the service is exactly right for the individual it is meant to be helping. This is of key significance, not just because it is a right to which everyone is entitled, but also because health and well-being respond to emotional factors as much as physical ones. Service users will benefit to a great extent if the service they receive is centred around their own needs and the ways in which they wish these needs to be met. Feeling valued as a person is likely to improve the self-esteem and self-confidence of service users and contribute to an overall improvement in their health and well-being.

When an individual either requests or is referred for a service, the assessment and planning cycle begins. Throughout the consultation and planning which follows, the individual and his or her needs should be at the centre of the process. You will need to make sure that the service user has every opportunity to state exactly how he or she wishes those needs to be met. Some service users will be able to give this information personally. Others will need an advocate who will support them in expressing their views.

The principles of good communication, which are explored in Unit 2, are an important part of making sure that the service user is fully involved in making plans for the service he or she will receive.

The consequences of not planning service delivery around the needs of those who receive it can be far reaching. The table below shows some of them.

Need/wish of service user	Ways to meet need	Possible effects of not taking account of need
Food prepared according to religious or cultural beliefs	Ensure that service is provided by people who have been trained to prepare food correctly	Food not eaten so health deteriorates. Other services refused Food eaten out of necessity but in extreme distress
To receive residential care but maintain social contacts	Provide transport to visit friends and for friends to visit	Service user becomes isolated and depressed
Take control of own arrangements for personal care	Discuss and support the planning of direct payments	Service user loses self-esteem and becomes disempowered

The impact of practising in a way which makes people feel valued is enormous. Often the steps are small and do not take a great deal of effort or demand major changes, but the results are so effective that any effort you have made will be repaid many times over by the benefits for the service users you care for.

Outcome activity 1.2

Welcome House is a resource centre providing residential and supported living accommodation along with community care for older people. It is in a city which has a very varied ethnic and racial make-up. Large numbers of people from many different cultural and racial backgrounds live in the area. Some have been there for many years, large numbers were born in the area and others have recently arrived in the country.

You have been asked to produce a guide which will help new service users at Welcome House and also new members of staff to become familiar with facilities in the area. You can do this alone, but it is better if you can work in a small group.

Step 1

Plan how to produce your guide. You could produce a paper booklet or information folder, word processed and with illustrations, or you could produce an on-line guide on a computer. You will need to make sure that the format you choose is accessible for the people who may use the guide.

After deciding on the format of your guide, decide what to include in it. Remember that this is for staff as well as service users, so you must make sure that you provide information which is useful for both groups; some information may be the same, but you will need to work out what different information may be needed.

Step 2

Carry out the research for your guide. You will need to find out about the different needs of people who come from different cultural and racial backgrounds. As you are describing an imaginary setting, you could check out the local facilities in your own area so that you can include their features in your guide. Clearly identify where the facilities are and how to access them. You may choose to do this on a map or by producing a list.

Step 3

Produce your guide using the planned format. When it is complete, show it to your supervisor, tutor and assessor and, if possible, to service users and ask for their feedback on how useful they think it would be.

How to recognise your own prejudices

One of the hardest things to do is to acknowledge the prejudices which are part of your own values and beliefs, and how they affect what you do. Prejudices may often come into conflict with the situations you work in. There is nothing wrong with having your own beliefs and values – everyone has them, and they are a vital part of making you the person you are. But you must be aware of them, and how they may affect what you do at work.

Think about the basic principles which apply in your life. For example, you may have a basic belief that you should always be honest. Then think about what that could mean for the way you work – might you find it hard to be pleasant to someone who was found to have lied extensively? You may believe that abortion is wrong. Could you deal sympathetically with a woman who had had an abortion? You may have been brought up to take great care of people with disabilities and believe that they should be looked after and protected. How would you cope in an environment which encouraged people with disabilities to take risks and promoted their independence?

Check it out

Make a list of the things you believe in as values, and a second list of how they could affect your work. Then examine whether they do affect your work – you may need the views of a trusted colleague or your supervisor to help you with this. This exercise is very hard, and it will take a long time to do. It is often better done over a period of time. As you become more aware of your own actions, you will notice how they have the potential to affect your work.

Once you are aware of your own beliefs and values, and have recognised how important they are, you must think about how to accept the beliefs and values of others. The individuals you work with are all different, and so it is important to recognise and accept that diversity.

In a previous outcome, you looked at the rights which people can exercise under the law. This outcome is concerned with understanding the varied nature of human beings and how to ensure that the differences are valued and acknowledged.

Many workplaces now have policies which are about 'Managing Diversity' rather than 'Equal Opportunities'. This is because many people have realised that until diversity is recognised and valued, there is no realistic possibility of any policy about equal opportunities being totally effective.

1 This exercise is best done with a group of colleagues, but you can do it on your own – it just takes longer! Think of some ideas for a list of all the cultures and nationalities you know of. Write them down. Next to each one, write something that the culture has given to the world. For example, the Egyptians gave mathematics, the Chinese developed some wonderful medicines, and so on.

2 Next, think about people from the groups you care for. Note down the special angle of understanding each group can bring to society. For instance, someone who is visually impaired will always judge people on how they behave, not on how they look. Older people can often bring a different perspective to a situation based on years of experience and understanding.

3 In your own workplace, find out about the policy for ensuring equal opportunities, or for managing diversity. Make sure you read the policy. Consider whether you think it is being implemented.

What is anti-discriminatory and anti-oppressive practice?

Anti-discriminatory practice is what underpins the work in care settings. You, as a care worker, must practise in an anti-discriminatory way in your day-to-day work with service users. In order to be able to practise in a way which opposes discrimination, you must first understand the main concepts involved. You are likely to find that you have come across these ideas before, but perhaps not in these terms or in this context. You will need to understand the terms, because you will hear them used throughout the care and related sectors, and they have important implications for your practice.

Stereotyping	Stereotyping is happening when whole groups of people are assumed to be the same. It is often present when you hear phrases such as 'these sorts of people all ...'.
	'Old people love a sing song' or 'black people are good athletes' or 'gypsies are all dirty and up to no good' are all stereotyping remarks.
Labelling	Slightly more complex than stereotyping, labelling happens when someone thinks the factor which people have in common is more important than the hundreds of factors which make them different.

	For example, the remark 'We should organise a concert for the elderly' makes an assumption that being older is what is important about the people concerned, and that somehow as you grow older your tastes become the same as all other people your age! It would be much better to say 'We should organise a concert for older people who like music from the shows' or 'We should organise a concert for older people who like opera', etc.
Discrimination	Discrimination means treating people less favourably because they have a feature or characteristic, over which they have no control. Disabled people find it hard to get a job because employers are reluctant to take them on. Research has shown that people with Asian names or from certain areas are told that job vacancies have been filled even though they have not. Disabled people are often unable to go to concerts or eat in the restaurants they want to because there are no suitable facilities for them.
Anti-discrimination	This means positively working to eliminate discrimination. It is about more than being against discrimination. You must ensure through your practice that you protect service users from discrimination by identifying it and taking steps to get rid of it or reduce it wherever you can. For example, when weekly menus are being planned at a day centre, if no account is taken of the religious and cultural needs of all the service users, you should raise the issue at a staff meeting and suggest changes.
Oppression	Oppression is the experience people have when they are discriminated against. People who are oppressed are being prevented from receiving equal treatment and exercising their rights. People who are oppressed often lose self-confidence and find it difficult to see a way to change the treatment they are subjected to.
Anti-oppression	This is about the practical steps you can take to counteract oppression. In your work setting you will need to make sure that service users have all the information and support they need to understand the rights they have and how to exercise them. This may mean finding out about what they are entitled to and the ways in which they can be helped, setting up appointments for them and providing written information. It can also mean offering emotional support. It is important to recognise when people are being oppressed and denied their rights, either by another individual or by an organisation. You must work to challenge this, or support service users in challenging it for themselves.

Check it out

Find an example of each of the aspects of anti-discriminatory practice. The examples can be from work, or from other parts of your life, or from fiction (a book, film or TV programme). For each example look at what you can learn about working in a way which is anti-discriminatory.

Your day-to-day practice and attitudes are important in how effective your anti-discriminatory practice will be. There is little point in challenging stereotyping in support of a service user, and then returning to your own work setting ready to organise all the 'ladies' for a sewing afternoon!

Challenging your own prejudices and attitudes can be difficult, but you need to spend some time checking out your own behaviour, and making sure that you are not guilty of some of the discriminatory behaviour you have been challenging in others. Exploring your own behaviour is never easy, and you need good support either from your supervisor or close friends to do it. You may be upset by what you find out about some of your attitudes, but knowing about them and acknowledging them is the first step to doing something about them.

As a care worker, it will be easier to make sure that you are practising effectively if you are confident that you have looked at your own work and the attitudes which underpin it.

Getting feedback

It is sometimes difficult to take a step back and look at whether your working practices have improved as a result of training, development and increasing experience. So it is very important to seek out and act on feedback from an appropriate person, usually your supervisor.

Mirror, mirror on the wall...

Asking for feedback on your performance is not always easy – and listening to it can be harder! All of us find it difficult to hear feedback at times, especially if we are being told we could do things better. However, you should learn to welcome feedback. Try to think of it as looking in a mirror. You probably never go out without looking in the mirror to check how you look. Think of professional feedback in the same way – how will you know how you are performing if you haven't asked anyone who is in a position to tell you?

Don't forget that you can ask for feedback from service users and colleagues too, not only from your supervisor.

Quality working

It is only by regularly evaluating your own practice that you can be sure you are working to the highest possible standards, and meeting all the requirements for quality provision, such as those laid out in national standards.

The central theme and underpinning principle of care provision is that the service is centred on the person receiving it, and not on those providing it. The Care Standards Act 2000 put into law the concept of monitoring and regulating service providers to make sure that services are meeting the needs of the individuals for whom they are provided.

The Act established the National Care Standards Commission, which is responsible for implementing the National Minimum Standards across a wide range of care providers. The Commission inspects and regulates over 40,000 different establishments. Each type of care provider has a set of National Minimum Standards which it must meet, and against which it is regularly inspected.

In this way, service users are assured that the service they receive is of good quality, and also that all those working in care settings have standards of performance. These are laid out in the National Occupational Standards which form the basis of the National Vocational Qualifications (NVQs).

Outcome activity 1.3

Over a period of two weeks, collect at least six newspaper or magazine cuttings, or print out items from web-based news sites, about controversial or difficult issues. The cuttings can be about anything which has caught your interest – they do not have to be related to care, but they can be. Three of the cuttings must be articles which you agree with or think are right. Three of the cuttings must be items which describe actions or attitudes you disagree with or think are wrong. Go through each of your cuttings carefully and work out the reasons why you agreed or disagreed with the content.

The next steps should be carried out in a small group. If you are not working with a group of other candidates, then ask your supervisor, assessor or work colleagues to help you.

Step 1
Working in a small group, each person should identify a cutting he or she agrees with and explain to the group why. Each should then identify a cutting that he or she disagrees with and explain the reasons. Continue until all the cuttings have been considered.

Step 2
As a group, discuss the cuttings and look at the different reasons for agreement and disagreement. One person in the group should keep notes about the subjects discussed and the views expressed.

Step 3
On your own, prepare a reflective account on what this exercise has shown you about why you hold the values and beliefs you do. Include the following in the account:

▶ the values and beliefs you identified
▶ any which may seem to contradict each other – for example, you may believe in equal opportunities, but think that people seeking political asylum should not be allowed into the country
▶ what you learned about the influences on your values and beliefs
▶ the effects you think your own values and beliefs could have on the work you do.

Step 4
Share your account with your group and tutor or supervisor, and discuss the issues it raises.

The principles of data protection

All information, however it is stored, is subject to the rules laid down in the Data Protection Act 1998, which covers medical records, social service records, credit information, local authority information – in fact, anything which is personal data (facts and opinions about an individual).

Anyone processing personal data must comply with the eight principles of good practice. These say that data must be:

▶ fairly and lawfully processed
▶ processed for limited purposes
▶ adequate, relevant and not excessive
▶ accurate
▶ not kept for longer than necessary
▶ processed in accordance with the data subject's rights
▶ kept secure
▶ not transferred to countries without proper protection.

Who can see confidential records?

Every health and caring organisation has a policy on confidentiality and the disclosure of information. You must be sure that you know what the policies are in your workplace.

The basic rule is that all the information an individual gives, or that is given on his or her behalf, to an organisation is confidential and cannot be disclosed to anyone without the consent of the individual.

Passing on information

In many cases, the passing of information is routine and related to the care of the individual. For example, medical information may be passed to a hospital, to a residential home or to a private care agency. It must be made clear to the individual that this information will be passed on in order to ensure that he or she receives the best possible care.

The key thing to remember is that only the information which is required for the purpose is passed on. For example, it is not necessary to tell the hearing aid clinic that Mr S's son is currently serving a prison sentence. However, if he became seriously ill and the hospital wanted to contact his next of kin, that information would need to be passed on.

Each organisation should have a policy which states clearly the circumstances in which information can be disclosed. According to government guidelines ('Confidentiality of Personal Information', 1988) the policy should state:

▶ the identity of the senior managers who deal with decisions about disclosing information
▶ what to do when urgent action is required
▶ what safeguards are in place to make sure that the information will be used only for proper purposes
▶ the arrangements for obtaining manual records and computer records
▶ the arrangements for reviewing the procedure.

When you need to break confidentiality

There are several reasons why information may need to be disclosed without consent. The individual should be informed about what has been disclosed at the earliest possible opportunity.

The one exception to this is where information is given in order to assist an investigation into suspected child abuse. In that case, the individual should not be told of any information which has been disclosed, until this has been agreed by those carrying out the investigation.

Information may be required by a tribunal, a court or by the ombudsman. Ideally it should be given with the service user's consent, but it will have to be provided regardless of whether the consent is given.

You may have to consider the protection of the community, if public health is at stake. For example, you may be aware that someone has an infectious illness, or is a carrier of such an illness and is putting people at risk. If someone was infected with salmonella, but still insisted on going to work in a restaurant kitchen, you would have a duty to inform the appropriate authorities.

There are other situations where you may need to give information to the police. If a serious crime is being investigated, the police can ask for information to be given. But information can only be requested in respect of a serious offence, and it has to be asked for by a senior officer, of at least the rank of superintendent. This means that if the local constable asks if you know whether Mr J has a history of mental health problems, you are not free to discuss the matter.

There may also be times when it is helpful to give information to the media. For example, an elderly confused man, who wanders regularly, may have gone missing. A description given out on the local radio and in the local paper may help to locate him before he comes to any serious harm.

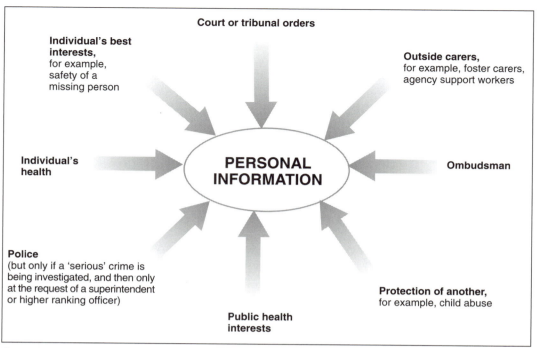

Some reasons why information may be disclosed without consent.

REMEMBER

Disclosure without consent is always a difficult choice. Your decision must be taken in consultation with your supervisor and in line with your organisation's policy. Remember the following main reasons why you may need to do this:

▶ if it is in the service user's interest
▶ if there is a serious risk to the community
▶ if there has been a serious crime, or if the risk of one exists
▶ in the case of an official/legal investigation.

There are other occasions when it is necessary to pass on information which has been given to you in confidence, or which an individual might expect you to keep confidential. One of the most difficult situations is where a child discloses to you that he or she is being abused. The best practice is to try not to get yourself in the position of agreeing to keep a secret.

Keys to good practice

✔ If you have been given information by a child concerning abuse, you have to pass on the information to your line manager, or whoever is named in the alerting procedures. This is not a matter of choice; even if the child refuses to agree, you have a duty to override his or her wishes. There are no circumstances in which disclosures of abuse of children must be kept confidential.

✔ The situation with an adult, perhaps an older person, who is being abused is different. You can only try to persuade him or her to allow you to pass on the information.

✔ You may be faced with information which indicates that someone intends to harm himself or herself. In that situation, you would be justified in breaking a confidence to prevent harm.

✔ If an individual is threatening to harm someone else, you should pass on the information immediately to your line manager, who will inform the police. It is not appropriate to contact the threatened person directly.

Check it out

Ask your manager about the confidentiality policy in your workplace. Find the procedure and make sure you know how to follow it.

People who need to know

It can be difficult when people claim to have a right or an interest in seeing an individual's records. Of course, there are always some people who do need to know, either because they are directly involved in providing care for the individual or because they are involved in some other support role. However, not everyone needs to know everything, so it is important that information is given on a 'need to know' basis. In other words, people are told what they need to know in order to carry out their role.

Relatives will often claim that they have a 'right to know'. The most famous example of this was Victoria Gillick, who went to court in order to try to gain access to her daughter's medical records. She claimed that she had the right to know if her daughter had been given the contraceptive pill. Her GP had refused to tell her and she took the case all the way to the House of Lords, but the ruling was not changed and she was not given access to her daughter's records. The rules remain the same. Even for close relatives, the information is not available unless the individual agrees.

It is difficult, however, if you are faced with angry or distressed relatives who believe that you have information they are entitled to. One situation you could encounter is where a daughter, for example, believes that she has the right to be told about medical information in respect of her parent. Another example is where someone is trying to find out a person's whereabouts. The best response is to be clear and assertive, but to demonstrate that you understand that it is difficult for them. Do not try to 'pass the buck' and give people the idea that they can find out from someone else. There is nothing more frustrating than being passed from one person to another without anyone being prepared to tell you anything. It is important to be clear and say something like, 'I'm sorry. I know you must be worried, but I can't discuss any information unless your mother agrees', or 'I'm sorry, I can't give out any information about where J is living now. But if you would like to leave me a name and contact details, I will pass on the message and she can contact you'.

Proof of identity

You should always check that people are who they claim to be. It is not unknown for newspaper reporters, unwanted visitors or even a nosey neighbour to claim that they are relatives or professionals from another agency. If basic precautions are not taken to confirm their identity, then they may be able to find out a great deal of confidential information.

In person

If you do not know the person who is claiming to have a right to be given information, you should:

▶ find out whether he or she is known to any of your colleagues
▶ ask for proof of identity – if he or she claims to be from another agency involved in providing care, he or she will have an official ID (identity card); otherwise ask for driving licence, bank cards, etc.

On the telephone

Unless you recognise the voice of the person, you should offer to take his or her telephone number and call back after you have checked.

If various members of the family or friends are likely to be telephoning about a particular service user, you could arrange a password.

REMEMBER

▶ Generally, you should only give information with consent.
▶ Only give people the information they need to know to do their job.
▶ Information should be relevant to the purpose for which it is required.
▶ Check the identity of the person to whom you give information.
▶ Make sure that you do not give information carelessly.

CASE STUDY

Mr R is 59 years old. He is a resident in a nursing home, and he is now very ill. He has Huntington's disease, which is a disease causing dementia, loss of mobility, and loss of speech. It is incurable and untreatable, and it is hereditary. Mr R was divorced many years ago when his children were very young and he has had no contact with his family for over 30 years.

A man who says he is Mr R's son comes to the nursing home in great distress. He is aware, through his mother, that his paternal grandfather died 'insane' and he has now heard about his father being in a nursing home. He is terrified that his father has a hereditary disease and that he also may have it. He has young children and is desperate to know if they are at risk.

1 What can you tell Mr R's son?
2 Does he have a right to know?
3 What do you think should happen?
4 Whose rights are your concern?

Looking after information

Once something is written down or entered on a computer, it becomes a permanent record. For this reason, you must be very careful what you do with any files, charts, notes or other written records. They must always be stored somewhere locked and safe. You need to be very careful with files which leave the workplace. There are many stories about files being stolen from cars or left on buses!

Records kept on computers must also be kept safe and protected. Your workplace will have policies relating to records on computers, which will include access being restricted by a password, and the computer system being protected against the possibility of people 'hacking' into it.

Computer records must be surrounded by proper security.

Methods of looking after information

Imagine going into a record shop which has thousands of CDs stored in racks but in no recognisable order; they are not filed by the name of the artist, nor by the title of the album. Imagine how much time it would take to trace the particular album that you were looking for. Anything from Eminem to the Rolling Stones to Mantovani would be all jumbled together! This is exactly what it is like with a filing system – unless there is a system that is easily recognisable and allows people to trace files quickly and accurately, then it is impossible to use.

Records are stored in filing systems. These may be computerised or manual. All organisations have a filing system, and one of the first jobs you must undertake is to learn how to use it.

REMEMBER

Someone who uses an organisation's filing system incorrectly can soon cause chaos!

Some organisations have people who deal specifically with filing, and they do not allow untrained people to access the files. This is likely to be the case if you work for a large organisation, such as an NHS trust. Smaller agencies are likely to have a general filing system which everybody in the organisation has access to and uses directly. This is exactly the kind of situation where files and records are likely to go missing and to be misplaced.

If you learn to appreciate the importance of records and the different systems that can be used for their storage, then you can assist rather than hinder the process of keeping records up to date, in the right place and readily accessible when people need them.

Computerised systems

Your organisation is likely to use a computerised system, and there will be very clear procedures which must be followed by everybody who accesses the system. The procedures will vary depending on the system used, but usually involve accessing files through a special programme, which may well have been written especially for your organisation, or be specifically for record-keeping in health and care.

You are unlikely to be able to delete or alter any information which is in someone's file on a computer. It is possible that you will only be able to add information in very specific places, or it could be that files are 'read only' and you cannot add any information to them. This process, because it will not allow people to change or alter files, does have the advantage that information is likely to remain in a clear format. It is less likely to become lost or damaged in the way that manual files are. After all, it is really not possible to leave a computer system on a bus!

A computerised system enables organisations to keep a great deal more information in much less space. Although they can be expensive initially to install and to set up, the advantages outweigh the disadvantages in the long run. It also means that everybody in the organisation has to learn how to operate the system and how to use the computer – this is a new skill for a great many people! It is, however, a skill worth learning if it enables you to record and use information more accurately and effectively.

Manual systems

In a manual filing system the types of file used can vary. The most usual type of file is a manila folder with a series of documents fastened inside. Other types include ring binders, lever arch files and bound copies of computer printouts.

All of the files have to be organised (indexed) and stored in a way which makes them easily accessible whenever they are required.

Alphabetical systems

If there are not too many files, they can be kept in an alphabetical system in a simple filing cabinet or cupboard. In this sort of system, files are simply placed

according to the surname of the person they are about. They are put in the same order as you would see names in a telephone directory, starting with A and working through to the end of the alphabet, with names beginning *Mc* being filed like *Mac* and *St* being filed as *Saint*.

GPs' patient records can be kept using an alphabetical system, but most surgeries make extensive use of computer systems.

An alphabetical card index.

Numerical systems

Where there are large numbers of files an alphabetical system would not work. Imagine the numbers of M. Johnsons or P. Williams who would appear as

patients in a large hospital! In that situation an alphabetical filing system would become impossible to manage, so large organisations give their files numbers, and they are stored in number order. Clearly, a numerical system needs to have an index system so that a person's name can be attached to the appropriate number.

A hospital is likely to give a patient a number which will appear on all relevant documentation so that it is always possible to trace his or her medical notes. However, there still needs to be an overall record to attach that person's name and address to that particular set of case notes, and these days this is normally kept on a central computer which also records all prescriptions and test results.

Other indexing systems

It could be that, instead of files being organised alphabetically, they may be organised according to the different services an agency offers. For example, they could be kept under 'Mental health services', 'Care in the community services', 'Services for children' and so on. Within these categories files would be kept in alphabetical order. In a similar way, files may be organised under geographical areas.

Check it out

Find out about the filing system used in your workplace. Check how much information is kept in files, and how much on computer. Find out if the system is alphabetical or numerical, and ask someone who understands it to show you how to use it.

Outcome activity 1.4

Busyplace Health Resource Centre is a new, open-plan building which includes two GP practices, each with three doctors; a team of six health visitors; four community midwives; a counsellor; a community occupational therapist; and an outreach office for social services. There is also a voluntary services office which is used on different days by Victim Support, the National Childbirth Trust, the Asthma Society, the Diabetic Association, the Stroke Association, the local Citizens Advice Bureau and Relate. An administration section provides administrative support for all of the services in the centre.

The different services which operate in the centre keep records and information about all of the service users who access their facilities. One of the key features of the centre is that it provides a 'one-stop shop' so that people can find a wide range of help in one place. Many people use more than one of the centre's services.

All of the services based in the centre liaise with outside agencies, such as hospitals, residential establishments, supported living units, other professionals, the police, schools and colleges, support agencies, welfare and benefits providers, nursing agencies, and community development projects.

Your task is to prepare a checklist of all the aspects of confidential record-keeping which would apply in Busyplace Health Resource Centre. You can do this activity on your own, or working in a small group.

Step 1
Think about the different types of records which may be kept at the centre and make notes of them all.

Step 2

Read the information on Busyplace carefully. Make notes of any Acts of Parliament or guidelines you think may apply to the centre.

Step 3

Consider who may need access to any of the records or information held at the centre. Think about the people who may need to share information. Make notes of all of them.

Step 4

Prepare your checklist using the following headings. You could do this as a table on a computer:

Type of record/information	Relevant Act of Parliament/ guidelines	People who may need to access/ share information

Apply the principles of good communication and relationship building to care practice

Working in care is about communication and relationships. It is simply not possible to provide care services without developing good relationships with those you care for; and good communication is an essential part of relationship building whatever the nature of the relationship – a personal or family relationship, or a professional one.

Communication is about much more than just talking. It includes the messages you give out by your body language, and there are also a wide range of methods of communication ranging from telephones to text messages.

You will also need to think about the different ways in which people communicate and the barriers which some people face. Not everyone communicates in the same way and, as a professional care worker, you will need to be able to respond to a range of different ways of communicating.

This unit will help you to understand how all of these aspects of communication can be used in order to build and develop relationships and to improve your practice as a professional care worker.

Outcome 1: Apply the principles of effective communication with others

Why people communicate

In general, human beings like to live with other human beings. Most of us are sociable creatures who want to reach out to other people around us. Very few humans lead completely solitary lives. People live and communicate in a range of different groups and communities, for example:

- families
- neighbourhoods
- workplaces
- schools and colleges
- interest /activity groups
- commercial settings
- users of professional services.

The type and level of communication between people is very different, depending on the circumstances. Some communications are personal and very intimate. These are usually with people to whom we are very close.

Other communications are for a wider audience and are aimed at groups of people.

Communication can be formal.

Communication can be completely informal.

Check it out

Over a period of just one day, keep a record of the people you communicate with. Next to each name, write down the type of communication. You may find that most of your communication is informal, or mostly formal. For most of us, it will be a mix of the two.

Ways in which people communicate

This outcome is about how people reach out to each other. Communication is much more than talking. It is about how people respond to each other in many different ways: touch, facial expression, body movements, dress, position – and this is before you consider written communication, telephone, cyberspace, message in a bottle or pigeon!

REMEMBER

You are the most important tool you have for doing your job. Carers are not carefully engineered pieces of machinery or complex technology – your own ability to relate to others and to understand them is the key you need!

More than talking

Any relationship comes about through communication. In order to be an effective care worker, you must learn to be a good communicator. But communication is about much more than talking to people!

People communicate through:

▶ speaking
▶ facial expression
▶ body language
▶ position
▶ dress
▶ gestures.

You will have to know how to recognise what is being communicated to you, and be able to communicate with others without always having to use words.

Check it out

Do this with a friend or colleague.

1 Write the names of several emotions (such as anger, joy, sadness, disappointment, fear) on pieces of paper.
2 One of you should pick up a piece of paper. Your task is to communicate the emotion written on the paper to your partner, without saying anything.
3 Your partner then has to decide what the emotion is and say why.
4 Then change places and repeat the exercise. Take it in turns, until all the pieces of paper have been used. Make a list all the things which made you aware of the emotion being expressed.
5 Discuss with your partner what you have discovered about communication as a result of this exercise.

Key to good practice

When you carried out the last exercise, you probably found out that there are many things which tell you what someone is trying to communicate. It is not only the expression on people's faces which tells you about how they feel, but it is also the way they use the rest of their bodies. This area of human behaviour is referred to as non-verbal communication. It is a very important area for developing the ability to understand what people are feeling. If you understand the importance of non-verbal communication, you will be able to use it to improve your own skills when you communicate with someone.

Recognising signals

When you look at a person's facial expression, much of what you will see will be in his or her eyes, but the eyebrows and mouth are also important.

Notice whether someone is looking at you, or at the floor, or at a point over your shoulder. Lack of eye contact can give a first indication that all may not be well. It may be that the person is not feeling confident. He or she may be unhappy, or feel uneasy about talking to you. You will need to follow this up.

Look at how the person sits. Is he or she relaxed and comfortable, sitting well back in the chair, or tense and perched on the edge of the seat? Is he or she slumped in the chair, head down? Posture can indicate a great deal about how somebody is feeling. People who are feeling well and cheerful tend to hold their heads up, and sit in a relaxed and comfortable way. An individual who is tense and nervous, who feels unsure and worried, is likely to reflect that in the way he or she sits or stands.

Observe hands and gestures carefully. Someone twisting his or her hands, or playing with hair or clothes, is signalling tension and worry. Frequent little shrugs of the shoulders or spreading of the hands may indicate a feeling of helplessness or hopelessness.

CASE STUDY

Mrs B is very confused. She has little recognition of time or place and only knows her daughter, who has cared for her for many years. As she became increasingly frail and began to fall regularly, she finally stopped eating or drinking and her daughter had to arrange for her admission to hospital for assessment. She is in a large psycho-geriatric ward. Many of the patients are aggressive and disinhibited in their behaviour. Mrs B is quiet, gentle and confused, and she has no idea where she is. She does not know anyone, and she keeps asking to go home.

1 What would you expect Mrs B's body language to be?
2 What would you look for in her facial expression?
3 As her carer, how do you think you might make her feel better?
4 How would you communicate with her?
5 How might you help her daughter?

DID YOU KNOW?

Research shows that people pay far more attention to facial expressions and tone of voice than they do to spoken words. For example, in one study, words contributed only 7 per cent towards the impression of whether or not someone was liked, tone of voice contributed 38 per cent and facial expression 55 per cent. The study also found that if there was a contradiction between facial expression and words, people believed the facial expression.

Giving out signals

Being aware of your own body language is just as important as understanding the person you are talking to.

Keys to good practice

✔ Make sure that you maintain eye contact with the person you are talking to, although you should avoid staring! Looking away occasionally is normal, but if you find yourself looking around the room, or watching others, then you are failing to give people the attention they deserve.

✔ Be aware of what you are doing and try to think why you are losing attention.

✔ Sit where you can be comfortably seen. Don't sit where someone has to turn in order to look at you.

✔ Sit a comfortable distance away – not so far that any sense of closeness is lost, but not so close that you 'invade their space'.

✔ Make sure that you are showing by your gestures that you are listening and interested in what they are saying – sitting half-turned away gives the message that you are not fully committed to what is being said.

✔ Folded arms or crossed legs can indicate that you are 'closed' rather than 'open' to what someone is expressing.

✔ Nodding your head will indicate that you are receptive and interested – but be careful not to overdo it and look like a nodding dog!

✔ Lean towards someone to show that you are interested in what they are saying. You can use leaning forward quite effectively at times when you want to

emphasise your interest or support. Then move backwards a little at times when the content is a little lighter.

✔ Using touch to communicate your caring and concern is often useful and appropriate. Many individuals find it comforting to have their hand held or stroked, or to have an arm around their shoulders.

✔ Be aware of a person's body language, which should tell you if he or she finds touch acceptable or not.

✔ Always err on the side of caution if you are unsure about what is acceptable in another culture. On the next page, you will look at issues about cultures in which touch is unacceptable.

✔ Think about age and gender in relation to touch. An older woman may be happy to have her hand held by a female carer, but may be uncomfortable with such a response from a man.

✔ Ensure that you are touching someone because you think it will comfort him or her, and not because you feel helpless and can't think of anything to say.

Check it out

Do this with at least one other person – two or three is even better.

1 Think of an incident or situation which is quite important and significant to you. Stand still in the middle of a room and begin to tell your partner about your significant incident.

2 Your partner should start at the edge of the room and slowly move closer and closer to you.

3 At the point where you feel comfortable talking to your partner, say 'Stop'. Mark this point and measure the distance from where you are standing.

4 Continue. At the point where you feel that your partner is too close, say 'Stop'. Mark this point and measure the distance from where you are standing.

5 Change places and repeat the exercise.

You may find that you and your partner(s) will have different distances at which you feel comfortable, but it is likely to be in the range of 3–5ft.

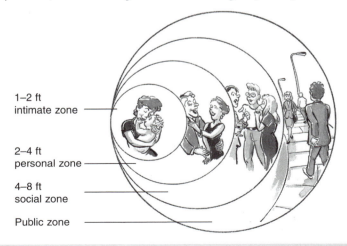

1–2 ft intimate zone

2–4 ft personal zone

4–8 ft social zone

Public zone

REMEMBER

▶ You can often learn as much by observing as by listening.

▶ Learn to 'listen with your eyes'.

▶ Your body sends out as many messages as the person you are talking to.

▶ Be aware of the messages you give to others.

Communication culture

Communication is about much more than words being exchanged between two people – it is influenced by a great many factors. The way in which people have been brought up and the society and culture that they live in have a great effect on the way in which they communicate.

People's communication differences can result from differences in culture and background. Culture is about more than language – it is about the way that people live, think and relate to each other.

For example, some cultures use gestures or touch much more than others. In some cultures it is acceptable to stand very close to someone, whereas in others people feel extremely uncomfortable if someone stands too close. You need to find out about the person's background when you are thinking about how you can make communication work for him or her. To find out the information you need, you could:

▶ look in the person's records

▶ speak to a member of the family or a friend, if this is possible

▶ ask someone else from the same culture, either a colleague or through the country's cultural representatives (contact the embassy or consulate and ask for the information) – alternatively you could try a local multicultural organisation

▶ use reference books, if necessary.

It is also important that you communicate with people at the correct intellectual level. Make sure that you communicate at a language level which people are likely to understand, but not find patronising. For example, older people and people who have disabilities have every right to be spoken to as adults and not patronised or talked down to. One of the commonest complaints from people with physical disabilities is that people will talk to their carers about them rather than talk to them directly – this is known as the 'does he take sugar' approach.

Hello Jane. How is he today? Is his cold better?

Overcoming cultural differences in communication

You will need to be aware of cultural differences between you and the person you are talking to. For example, using first names or touching someone to whom you are not related, or a very close friend, can be viewed as disrespectful in some cultures. Talking familiarly to someone of a different gender or age group can be unacceptable in some cultures. For example, some young Muslim women do not talk at all to men to whom they are not related.

Many older men and women consider it disrespectful to address people by their first names. You will often find older people with neighbours they have known for 50 years, who still call each other 'Mrs Baker' or 'Mrs Wood'.

Some people may have been brought up in a background or in a period of time when challenging authority by asking questions was not acceptable. Such people may find it very hard to ask questions of doctors or other health professionals, and are unlikely to feel able to raise any queries about how their care or treatment should be carried out.

REMEMBER

The golden rule when you are communicating with someone from a different culture is to *find out*. Do not assume that you can approach everyone in the same way. It is your responsibility to find out the way to approach someone.

What words mean

Be aware that the words you use can mean different things to different people and generations – words like 'cool', 'chip' or 'gay'. Be aware of particular local words which are used in your part of the country, which may not mean the same to someone from another area.

Think carefully about the subject under discussion. Some people from particular cultures, or people of particular generations, may find some subjects very sensitive and difficult to discuss. These days, it is not unusual among a younger age group to discuss personal income levels. However, people of older generations may consider such information to be highly personal.

What makes communication different?

Language

Where an individual speaks a different language from those who are providing care, it can be an isolating and frustrating experience. The individual may become distressed and frightened as it is very difficult to establish exactly what is happening and he or she is not in a position to ask or to have any questions answered. The person will feel excluded from anything happening in the care setting and will find making relationships with carers extremely difficult. There is the possibility that confusion and misunderstanding will occur.

Hearing loss

A loss or reduction of ability to hear clearly can cause major differences in the ability to communicate.

Communication is a two-way process, and it is very difficult for somebody who does not hear sounds at all or hears them in a blurred and indistinct way to be able to respond and to join in. The result can be that people become withdrawn and feel very isolated and excluded from others around them. This can lead to frustration and anger. As a result, people may present some quite challenging behaviour.

Profound deafness is not as common as partial hearing loss. People are most likely to suffer from loss of hearing of certain sounds at certain volumes or at certain pitches, such as high sounds or low sounds. It is also very common for people to find it difficult to hear if there is background noise – many sounds may jumble together, making it very hard to pick out the voice of one person. Hearing loss can also have an effect on speech, particularly for those who are profoundly deaf and are unable to hear their own voices as they speak. This can make communication doubly difficult.

Visual impairment

Visual impairment causes many communication difficulties. Not only is an individual unable to pick up the visual signals which are being given out by someone who is speaking, but, because he or she is unaware of these signals, the person may also fail to give appropriate signals in communication. This lack of non-verbal communication can lead to misunderstandings about somebody's attitudes and behaviour. It means that a person's communications can easily be misinterpreted, or it could be thought that he or she is behaving in a way that is not appropriate.

Physical disability

Depending on the disability, this can have various effects. People who have suffered strokes, for example, will often have communication difficulties, not only in forming words and speaking, but they often also suffer from aphasia (or dysphasia), which is the inability to understand and to express meaning through words. They lose the ability to find the right words for something they want to say, or to understand the meanings of words said to them. This condition is very distressing for the individual and for those who are trying to communicate. Often this is coupled with a loss of movement and a difficulty in using facial muscles to form words.

In some cases, the communication difficulty is a symptom of a disability. For example, many people with cerebral palsy and motor neurone disease have difficulty in controlling the muscles that affect voice production, and so speaking in a way which can be readily understood becomes very difficult. Other disabilities may have no effect at all upon voice production or the thought processes that produce spoken words, but the lack of other body movements may mean that non-verbal communication may be difficult or not what you would expect.

Learning disabilities

These may, depending upon their severity, cause differences in communication in terms of the level of understanding of the individual and his or her ability to respond appropriately to any form of communication. This will vary depending on the degree of learning disability, but broadly the effect of learning disabilities is to limit the ability of an individual to understand and process information given to him or her. It is also possible that individuals will have a short attention span, so this may mean that communications have to be repeated several times in an appropriate form.

Dementia/confusion

This difficult and distressing condition is most prevalent in older people and people who suffer from Alzheimer's disease. The confusion can result ultimately in the loss of the ability to communicate, but in the early stages it involves short-term memory loss to the extent of being unable to remember the essential parts of a conversation or a recent exchange. It can mean that you must constantly repeat any form of communication.

Barriers to communication

On many occasions there are barriers to overcome before any effective communication can take place. Barriers can exist for all sorts of reasons – some to do with the physical environment, some to do with the background and circumstances of the service user, and some to do with the approach of the care worker.

The first barriers to check out are those which you could be creating yourself. You may think that you are doing everything possible to assist communication, but be sure that you are not making it difficult for service users to understand what you say.

As a professional care worker, you will use all kinds of quick ways to speak with colleagues. Using initials (acronyms) to refer to things is one of the commonest ways in which professionals use shortcuts when talking to each other. Some acronyms are commonplace and others are particular to that work setting. Often, particular forms or documents are referred to by initials – this is obviously useful in one workplace, but not in any others! Referring to medical conditions, types of medication, therapies or activities by initials or by using professional jargon can make it difficult for service users to understand, because these are words they don't use every day. Many of us would have difficulty following the explanation of a mechanic as to what was wrong with a car if he or she used only technical words and jargon. Similarly, service users and their families may have difficulty following care workers' communication. It is not that unusual to hear something like this:

Right – we've checked your BP – that's fine, your Hb came back OK so that means we can do an RF down to Gill our OT – she'll come and see you then fill out a 370 – that'll go to social services who'll send a CCM out to do an assessment and formulate a plan – OK?

It may have been more useful to say:

Your blood pressure is fine. The blood test showed that you're not anaemic, so that means that you're well enough for us to contact Gill, the occupational therapist. She will see you and assess what you can do and what help you may need. After that she'll contact social services and one of the community care managers will visit you to talk about the help and support you would like to have.

It takes a little longer, but saves time and confusion in the long run.

Some barriers to communication can be caused by failing to follow some of the steps towards good communication:

- ▶ not giving people proper space and time to say the things they want to say
- ▶ sitting in a noisy or crowded place
- ▶ sitting too far away or invading personal space
- ▶ having poor or unwelcoming body language.

Pushing down the barriers

There are many factors which can get in the way of good communication. You will need to understand how to recognise these and to learn what you can do to overcome them. Until you do this, your communication will always be less effective than it could be. It is easy to assume that everyone can communicate, and that any failure to respond to you is because of someone's unwillingness rather than inability. There are as many reasons why people find communication difficult as there are ways to make it easier.

Check it out

Choose two different ways in which you communicate with people, for example talking, writing, telephone, e-mail – you can probably think of others. Consider the most important element in each one. For example, for talking it could be language, for telephone, hearing, and so on. Now think about how you would manage that communication without that important element. List the problems you would have and the ways you could try to overcome them. Do you begin to see how difficult it can be sometimes for people to communicate?

Thinking about the obstacles

Never assume that you can be heard and understood and that you can be responded to, without first thinking about the individual and his or her situation. Check first to ensure you are giving the communication the best possible chance of success by dealing with as many barriers as possible.

If you need to communicate with someone who has a known disability, such as hearing loss, impaired vision, mobility problems or speech impairment, you must consider the implications for your communication.

Checklist

Practical difficulties ✓

Cultural difficulties ✓

What words mean ✗

Physical barriers ✓

Hearing loss

If someone is profoundly deaf, you will need to establish what sort of assistance he or she needs. If he or she communicates by signing, you will need to have a sign language interpreter available. Do not assume that you can do this yourself – it is highly skilled and people train for a long time to do this. If someone uses a hearing aid, consider that it may not be operating efficiently if you seem to be having communication problems.

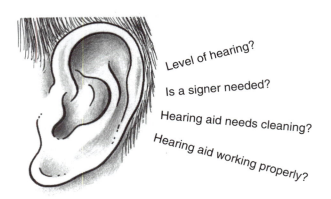

Level of hearing?

Is a signer needed?

Hearing aid needs cleaning?

Hearing aid working properly?

Consider the level of someone's hearing. Many people are hard of hearing, but this may not be a profound hearing loss. It can mean that they have difficulty hearing where there is background noise and other people talking.

The areas to think about when planning communication with someone with hearing loss are the following.

▶ Ensure that any means for improving hearing that is in use, for example a hearing aid, is working properly and is fitted correctly, that the batteries are fresh and working, that it is clean and that it is doing its job properly in terms of improving the individual's hearing.

▶ Ensure that you are sitting in a good light, not too far away and that you speak clearly, but do not shout. Shouting simply distorts your face and makes it more difficult for a person with hearing loss to be able to read what you are saying.

Some people will lip read, while others will use a form of sign language for understanding. This may be BSL (British Sign Language) or MAKATON, which uses signs and symbols. They may rely on a combination of lip reading and gestures.

REMEMBER

If you are able to learn even simple signing or the basic rules of straightforward spoken communication with people who have hearing loss, you will significantly improve the way in which they are able to relate to their care environment.

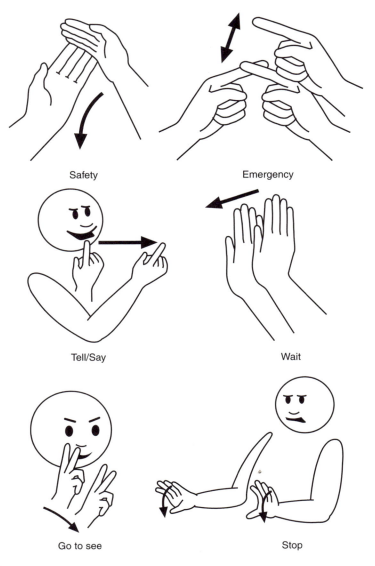

Safety

Emergency

Tell/Say

Wait

Go to see

Stop

BSL signs.

Other services which are extremely helpful to people who have hearing difficulties are telecommunication services, such as using a minicom or typetalk service. These allow a spoken conversation to be translated into written form using a form of typewriter, and the responses can be passed in the same way by an operator who will relay them to the hearing person. These services have provided a major advance in enabling people who are hard of hearing or profoundly deaf to use telephone equipment. For people who are less severely affected by hearing impairment there are facilities such as raising the volume on telephone receivers to allow them to hear conversations more clearly.

CASE STUDY

Mr T lives alone. For many years he has been well known in the neighbourhood. He was never particularly chatty, but always said a polite 'Good Morning' on his way to the shops, and had a smile and a kind word for the children. His wife died about 15 years ago. They had only one son, and he has also died.

Recently, Mr T's health has begun to deteriorate. He had a bad winter with a chest infection and a nasty fall in the snow. This seemed to shake his confidence, and he accepted the offer of a home-care assistant twice each week.

Neighbours began to notice that Mr T no longer spoke to them, and he failed to acknowledge the children. His outings to the shops became less frequent. Jean, his home-care assistant, was worried that he hardly responded to her cheerful chat as she worked. She realised that Mr T's hearing was deteriorating. After medical investigations, Mr T was provided with a hearing aid. He began to be much more like his old self – he spoke to people again, smiled at the children and enjoyed his visits to the shops.

1 How do you think Mr T felt when he began to have problems hearing people?
2 Why do you think he reacted in the way he did?
3 What other factors might Jean have thought were causing Mr T's deterioration?
4 How are people likely to have reacted to Mr T?

Visual impairment

Individuals who have vision which is impaired to any significant degree will need to be addressed with thought and care. Do not rely on your facial expressions to communicate your interest and concern – use words and touch where appropriate. Remember to obtain any information that may be needed in a format they can use. Think about large-print books, braille or audio tapes. If you need any further information, the Royal National Institute for the Blind (RNIB) will be able to advise you about local sources of supplies.

One of the commonest ways of assisting people who have impaired vision is to provide them with glasses or contact lenses. You need to be sure that these are clean and that they are the correct prescription. You must make sure that people have their eyes tested every two years and that their prescription is regularly updated. A person whose eyesight and requirements for glasses have changed will obviously have difficulty in picking

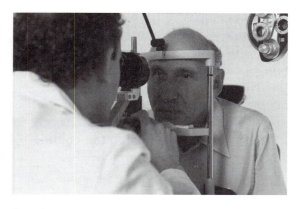
People should have their eyes tested every two years and their prescription should be regularly updated.

up many of the non-verbal signals which you will be giving out when you are communicating with him or her.

For people with more serious loss or impairment, you will need to take other steps to ensure that you minimise the differences that will exist in your styles of communication.

Keys to good practice

When communicating with people who have impaired vision:

✔ Do not suddenly begin to speak to someone without first of all letting him or her know that you are there by touching and saying hello.

✔ Make sure that you introduce yourself when you come into a room. It is easy to forget that someone cannot see. A simple 'hello John, it's Sue' is all that is needed so that you don't 'arrive' unexpectedly.

✔ You may need to use touch more than you would in speaking to a sighted person, because the concerns that you will be expressing through your face and your general body movements will not be seen. So, if you are expressing concern or sympathy, it may be appropriate to touch someone's hand or arm, at the same time that you are saying you are concerned and sympathetic.

✔ Ask the individual what system of communication he or she requires – do not impose your idea of appropriate systems on the person. Most people who are visually impaired know very well what they can and cannot do, and if you ask they will tell you exactly what they need you to do.

✔ Do not decide that you know the best way to help. Never take the arm of somebody who is visually impaired to help him or her to move around. Allow the person to take your arm or shoulder, to be guided and tell you where he or she wishes to go.

Language differences

Make sure that you know what language an individual is comfortable with – do not assume it is the same as yours without making certain! Find out if you need to provide any translation facilities, or written information in another language.

Where you are in the position of providing care for someone who speaks a different language from you, it is clear that you will need the services of an interpreter for any serious discussions or communication.

▶ Your work setting is likely to have a contact list of interpreters.
▶ Social services departments and the police have lists of interpreters.
▶ The embassy or consulate for the appropriate country will also have a list of qualified interpreters.

You should always use professional interpreters wherever possible. It may be very tempting to use other members of the family – very often children have excellent language skills – but it is inappropriate in most care settings. This is because:

▶ their English and their ability to interpret may not be at the same standard as a professional interpreter, and misunderstandings can easily occur
▶ you may wish to discuss matters which are not appropriate to be discussed with children, or the individual may not want members of his or her family involved in very personal discussions about health or care issues.

It is unlikely that you would be able to have a full-time interpreter available throughout somebody's period of care, so it is necessary to consider alternatives for encouraging everyday communication.

Be prepared to learn words in the individual's language which will help communication. You could try to give the person some words in your language if he or she is willing and able to learn them.

There are other simple techniques that you may wish to try which can help basic levels of communication. For example, you could use flashcards and signals, similar to those which you would use for a person who has suffered a stroke. This gives the person the opportunity to show a flashcard to indicate his or her needs. You can also use them to find out what kind of assistance may be needed.

Some of the flashcards you may use.

You will come up with many ideas for flashcards which are appropriate for the individual and for your particular care setting. They are a helpful way of assisting with simple communication and allowing people to express their immediate physical needs.

The most effective way of communicating with a person who speaks a different language is through non-verbal communication. A smile and a friendly face are understood in all languages, as are a concerned facial expression and a warm and welcoming body position.

However, be careful about the use of gestures – gestures which are acceptable in one culture may not be acceptable in all. For example, an extended thumb in some cultures would mean 'great, that's fine, OK', but in many cultures it is an extremely offensive gesture. If you are unsure which gestures are acceptable in another culture, make sure that you check before using any which may be misinterpreted.

Physical disability

If someone has a physical disability, you will need to consider whether this is likely to affect his or her non-verbal communication. Also, his or her body language may not be what you would expect.

Facial expressions may seem inappropriate

Hand and arm gestures may not be possible

Body posture may not give out the messages you would expect

Physical disability or illness has to be dealt with according to the nature of the disability or the illness. For example, if you were communicating with somebody who had a stroke you would have to work out ways of coping with his or her dysphasia. This is best dealt with by:

▶ using very simple, short sentences, speaking slowly and being prepared to wait while the individual processes what you have said and composes a reply
▶ using gestures – they are helpful in terms of making it easier for people to understand the idea that you are trying to get across
▶ using drawing, writing or flashcards to help understanding
▶ using very simple, closed questions which only need a 'yes' or 'no' answer. Avoid long, complicated sentences. For example, don't say 'It's getting near tea time now, isn't it? How about some tea? Have you thought about what

you would like?' Instead ask a series of simple questions: 'Are you hungry? Would you like fish? Would you like chicken?' and so on, until you have established what sort of meal the individual would prefer.

Other illnesses, such as motor neurone disease or cerebral palsy, can also lead to difficulties in speech, although not in comprehension.

▶ The individual will understand perfectly what you are saying to him or her but the difficulty will be in communicating with you.

▶ There is no need for you to speak slowly, although you will have to be prepared to allow time for a response owing to the difficulties that the individual will have in producing words.

▶ You will have to become familiar with the sound of the individual's voice and the way in which he or she communicates. It can be hard to understand people who have illnesses which affect their facial, throat or larynx muscles.

Learning disability

Where people have a learning disability, you will need to adjust your methods of communicating to take account of the level of disability that they experience. You should have gathered sufficient information about the individual to know the level of understanding that he or she has – and how simply and how often you need to explain things and the types of communication which are likely to be the most effective.

Many people with a learning disability respond well to physical contact and are able to relate and communicate on a physical level more easily than on a verbal level. This will vary between individuals, but you should be prepared to use a great deal of physical contact and hugs when communicating with people who have a learning disability.

Many people with a learning disability are able to communicate on a physical level more easily than on a verbal level.

Listening effectively

Communication is a two-way process. This may sound obvious, but a great deal of communication is wasted because only one of the parties is communicating. Think about setting up communication between two radios – when a link is established, the question is asked 'Are you receiving me?' and the answer comes back 'Receiving you loud and clear'. Unfortunately, human beings don't do this exercise before they talk to each other!

If no one is listening and receiving the information a person is trying to communicate, it is just a waste of time. Learning how to listen is a key task for anyone working in care.

You may think that you know how to listen and that it is something you do constantly. After all, you are hearing all sorts of noises all day long – but simply hearing sounds is not the same thing as actively listening.

Check it out

Think about a time you have talked to someone you felt was really interested in what you were saying and listening carefully to you. Try to note down what it was that made you so sure he or she was really listening. Did the fact you thought the person was really listening to you make it easier to talk?

For most people, feeling that someone is really listening makes a huge difference to how confident they feel about talking. You will need to learn about ways in which you can show people you are listening to what they are saying.

Using body language

Although you may think that you do most of your communicating by speaking, you may be surprised to learn that over 80% of what you communicate to others is understood without you speaking a word. Body language, or non-verbal communication, is the way in which we pick up most of the messages people are trying to give us – and some that they're not!

The way in which you use your body can convey messages about:

- ▶ your feelings
- ▶ your intentions
- ▶ your concern
- ▶ your attitudes
- ▶ your interest
- ▶ your attention.

The messages are made clear by such things as facial expression, or maintaining eye contact; sitting forward when you are listening; or having an open and relaxed posture.

REMEMBER

Body language backs up the words you use – or body language can make a liar of you!

Your body language will let people know that you are really listening to what they are saying. Practise your listening skills in just the same way you would practise any other skill – you can learn to listen well.

Always:

▶ look at the person who is talking to you
▶ maintain eye contact, but without staring
▶ nod your head to encourage the person to talk and show that you understand
▶ use 'aha', 'mm' and similar expressions which indicate that you are still listening
▶ lean slightly towards the person who is speaking – this indicates interest and concern
▶ have an open and interested facial expression, which should reflect the tone of the conversation – happy, serious, etc.

Using verbal communication

Body language is one key to effective listening, but what you say in reply is also important. You can back up the message that you are interested and listening by checking that you have understood what has been said to you. Using phrases beginning 'so …' to check that you have got it right can be helpful. 'So … it's only since you had the fall that you are feeling worried about being here alone.' 'So … you were happy with the service before the hours were changed.'

You can also use expressions such as 'So what you mean is …' or 'So what you are saying is …'

Short, encouraging phrases used while people are talking can show concern, understanding or sympathy. Phrases such as 'I see', 'Oh dear', 'Yes', or 'Go on' all give the speaker a clear indication that you are listening and want him or her to continue.

Using questions

Sometimes questions can be helpful to prompt someone who is talking, or to try to move a conversation forward. There are two different kinds of questions. Questions that can be answered with just 'yes' or 'no' are **closed questions**. 'Would you like to go out today?' is a closed question.

An **open question** needs more than 'yes' or 'no' to answer it. 'What is your favourite kind of outing?' is an open question. Open questions usually being with:

▶ what
▶ how
▶ why
▶ when
▶ where.

Depending on the conversation and the circumstances, either type of question may be appropriate. For example, if you are encouraging someone to talk because he or she has always been quiet, but has suddenly begun to open up, you are more likely to use open questions to encourage him or her to carry on talking. On the other hand, if you need factual information or you just want to confirm that you have understood what has been said to you, then you may need to ask closed questions.

Check it out

What type of question is each of the following:

▶ 'Are you feeling worried?'
▶ 'What sort of things worry you?'
▶ 'Do you want to join in the games tonight?'
▶ 'Is your daughter coming to visit?'
▶ 'Why were you cross with Marge this morning?'
▶ 'Were you cross with Marge this morning?'
▶ 'What have you got planned for when your daughter comes to visit?'
▶ 'Do you live here alone?'
▶ 'How do you feel about living alone?'

One of the main points to remember when listening is that whatever you say, there should not be too much of it! You are supposed to be listening, not speaking. Some DON'T's for good listening:

▶ Don't interrupt – always let people finish what they are saying, and wait for a gap in the conversation.
▶ Don't give advice – even if asked. You are not the person concerned, so you cannot respond to questions which start 'If you were me …'. Your job is to encourage people to take responsibility for their own decisions, not to tell them what to do!
▶ Don't tell people about your own experiences. Your own experiences are relevant to you because they teach you about the kind of person you are, but your role is to listen to others, not talk about yourself.
▶ Don't ever dismiss fears, worries or concerns by saying 'that's silly …' or 'you shouldn't worry about that'. People's fears are real and should not be made to sound trivial.

Check it out

Think about two particular occasions when you have been involved in communicating with service users. Write a brief description of the circumstances, and then write notes on how you showed the service users that you were listening to them. If you have not yet had enough experience of working with service users to be able to think of two occasions, think about times when you have listened effectively to a friend or relative and write about that instead.

Outcome activity 2.1

Communicating with others is an essential part of effective work in care, but communication may not always be straightforward. Work in pairs for this activity.

Step 1
Look again at the case study on page 58 and the questions which follow.

Step 2
Sit down with your partner and go through the answers you have decided upon, explaining why you have given them. You should plan to talk for at least 5 minutes. Your partner's job is to listen to you and to respond appropriately to what you are saying. Swap roles and listen to your partner doing the same thing.

Step 3
Make notes about how you felt when your partner was listening to you. Did you feel that he or she was interested? Were you encouraged to talk? Or did you feel rushed, or that he or she was not very interested?

Step 4
Give feedback to your partner on how well he or she listened to you, and have your partner give feedback to you.

Different types of relationships

Everyone has a wide range of relationships with different people in different aspects of their lives, ranging from family to work colleagues. Each of the different types of relationship is important and plays a valuable role in contributing to the overall well-being of each of us as an individual. However, the needs and demands of different types of relationships are varied, as are the effects that relationships can have on individuals' views of themselves and the confidence with which they deal with the world.

Types of relationships	Features of relationship
Family relationships	These are relationships with parents, grandparents, siblings and children. Depending on the type of family, they can be close or distant.
Sexual relationships	These relationships can be long term or short term. They can be with a spouse or permanent partner, or can be shorter-term non-permanent relationships. The impact of sexual relationships is different from family relationships and more intense than the demands of friendship.
Friendships	Friendships can be long term or can be short term but quite intense. Most people have a few close friends and a much larger circle of friends who are not quite so intimate or close. These may be friends who are part of a wide social circle, but not close enough to share intimate details. Close friends, on the other hand, are often the ones who are an immediate source of support in times of difficulty, and the first with whom good news is shared.
Working relationships	These can be relationships with employers or with work colleagues. Some may become friendships, but most people relate to work colleagues in a different way from the way they relate to friends. For example, work colleagues may share very little information about their personal lives even though they may have very close and regular day-to-day contact. It is perfectly possible to spend a great deal more time with work colleagues than with friends, but not to be as close.

Family relationships

Family relationships are usually those that influence people most. For most people the type of relationship they have within the family as they grow up influences the rest of their lives. Primarily it is the relationship with the parents or main carers which is the most influential during childhood. Relationships with parents, and other family members such as grandparents and siblings, provide the emotional security which is important in establishing a positive self-image and in developing confidence in a growing child. As children reach adolescence and early adulthood, family relationships become less dominant, but they do retain a great deal of significance for most people throughout their lives. It is notable that most of the major occasions in people's lives such as coming-of-age, weddings or christenings are regarded as family occasions and members of the immediate and extended family are usually involved in the celebrations.

Sexual relationships

Most people who have a long-term sexual relationship would probably view that as being the most significant relationship in their lives. Even short-term sexual relationships can have a huge effect on individuals and how they regard themselves and their general health and well-being.

The physical closeness involved in a sexual relationship means that the dynamics involved are significantly different from other family relationships. Sexual partners are often closer emotionally as a result of their intimate physical relationship. Sexual relationships can be long or short term, can be with an opposite or same sex partner, and can be exclusive (with just one partner) or non-exclusive (where partners also have relationships with others). These different types of relationships will obviously have different effects and will meet the needs of different individuals at different stages in their lives. For example, many teenagers and young adults have short-term and non-exclusive sexual relationships with a number of partners, but many will eventually develop a long-term exclusive relationship with one partner with whom they may remain for many years.

Friendships

Friends become increasingly significant as children grow. For very young and pre-school children, individual friendships with other children are relatively insignificant as an influence on their lives – their relationships with other members of the family, especially the main carer, are far more important. As children progress through school and into adolescence their friendships become of great importance and have a huge influence on their behaviour.

The ability to form friendships with others is an important skill and fulfils a need which most human beings have. An inability to make friends or a situation in which a child or young person feels friendless or is being bullied or excluded can be extremely distressing, and can have a serious effect on a child's self-image and self-confidence. Adults, too, find it difficult to be excluded and to be put in a situation where they are unable to relate to others. Most people, regardless of circumstances, need to have a close relationship with another person which will enable them to share confidences, worries and joys.

Working relationships

Effective working relationships are extremely important both to individuals and to the organisations for whom they work. Business managers use techniques which are designed to encourage work colleagues to work well and effectively together, and many companies spend a great deal of time and effort in building work teams.

Establishing good working relationships with colleagues usually requires an effective use of communication skills and a recognition of the value and significance of work undertaken by colleagues. For most people, having a good working relationship with colleagues is important as it contributes significantly to overall job satisfaction.

We all develop relationships that are important to our lives.

Features of relationships

All relationships are different and they will all have different aspects and features. Some features are positive and some are negative. It is important to establish the balance of features in a relationship to know whether it is positive or negative.

Some relationships may be:

▶ **Supportive** A professional carer's relationships with service users should be supportive, which means providing help, sympathy and positive benefits.
▶ **Sharing** Friendships or family relationships often include the sharing of both happiness and sadness.

- ▶ **Equal** Many friendships and many, but not all long-term sexual relationships are equal in that all parties feel valued and take equal responsibility for all aspects of the relationship. This could also apply to business partnerships.
- ▶ **Demanding** One of those in the relationship could be taking out more than he or she puts in, and making many demands.
- ▶ **Violent** Violence in a relationship is always an abuse of power – usually physical power, but it could be authority or emotional power.
- ▶ **Abusive** Abuse occurs where one of those in the relationship is exploiting another – either physically, sexually, emotionally, financially or by failing to provide care and nurture. Abuse arises out of misuse of power, as in a violent relationship.

Check it out

Think about three relationships you are part of. For each, describe the type of relationship, then look at the features of the relationship. Identify whether it is a positive or a negative relationship for you. Try to work out why you feel that it is positive or negative, and make a note of how you came to that conclusion.

Effects of relationships

Relationships have a significant effect on the development, health and well-being of all individuals. Most people like to be liked, and feel happy when they are part of a group or have friends. Very few people are content to be excluded from groups and to live in isolation without any significant close relationships. Generally, humans are sociable creatures who have always lived in groups, tribes or villages. Most are not loners, and their overall emotional health and well-being depends on the way they see themselves mirrored in the responses of others.

The professional caring relationship should provide support and encourage independence.

Professional caring relationships

As a professional working in a care setting, the relationships you form with service users and work colleagues are essential in providing an effective service.

You will need to make use of all the communication skills you have learned in order to develop relationships which make service users feel valued as individuals, respected and treated with dignity. The caring relationship must provide support and, most importantly, should empower the individual to become as independent as possible.

Working relationships with colleagues should be based on a professional respect for the skills and work of others, and consideration for the demands that work roles place on others. Workloads and responsibility should be shared as appropriate, and so should information and knowledge where this does not conflict with the principles of confidentiality.

Not all relationships and work will be plain sailing – you can find yourself having to deal with behaviour which is challenging and sometimes aggressive or even violent.

Challenging behaviour

People's behaviour is as much a means of communication as their facial expression or their words. If people are behaving in an unusual way or present you with a challenge, this tells you something of how they feel about what is going on around them.

You may find yourself dealing with behaviour which is new to you, or behaviour which you have seen before but with service users you have never met. The type of behaviour which can make relationships difficult can vary in different settings. Each workplace will have policies to deal with challenging behaviour, and you must make sure that your are familiar with them. You should also discuss with your supervisor the types of behaviour you are likely to come across in your workplace.

Many care workers have to deal with verbal abuse or aggression from service users. This may be related to anger and frustration, or it may be caused by the medical condition of the service user. Clearly, reasonable communication is not possible with someone who is being aggressive and abusive, and the situation needs to be calmed before communication can begin.

The basic rule is to follow the policies of your workplace in dealing with the particular behaviour, but do not be concerned about trying to communicate effectively until you have dealt with the behaviour and the situation is calm enough for communication to be possible.

Communication with people who are violently angry is difficult and, as a general rule, should be undertaken by highly experienced and skilled staff. If you find you are faced with this situation you should speak loudly (without shouting), firmly and clearly. Do not ask questions or enter into a discussion – you should issue short, clear instructions such as 'Stop shouting – now', 'Move way from Jim', ' Go and sit down', 'Go into my office' and so on. This type of short, firm instruction has a chance of defusing the situation and restoring enough calm for the problems to be investigated.

For more about ways to deal with challenging behaviour, see Unit 4, page 159.

Violent situations

There are some situations when verbal abuse and aggressive behaviour turn to violence, and this places you and service users at risk. You should never try to deal with a violent situation alone – you should always get help.

Always be alert to the situation you are in and take some common-sense precautions: make sure that you know where the exits are, and move so that the aggressor is not between you and the exit; notice if there is anything which could be used as a weapon, and try to move away from it; make sure that the aggressor has enough personal space, and do not crowd him or her.

If you are faced with a violent situation, you should try to remain calm (even though that is easier said than done!) and not resort to violence or aggression yourself.

It is often the case that a simple technique like holding up a hand in front of you, as if you were directing traffic, and shouting 'Stop' may deflect an attacker, or stop him or her long enough for you to get away. You should remove yourself from the situation as speedily as possible.

If there are other, vulnerable people at risk, you must decide whether you can summon help more effectively from outside or inside the situation.

If you decide to remain, you must summon help at once. You should do one of the following:

▶ press a panic alarm or buzzer, if one is provided
▶ shout 'help!' very loudly and continuously
▶ send someone for help
▶ call the police, or security, or shout for someone else to do so.

Do not try to be a hero – that is not your job.

Outcome activity 2.2

This activity will involve a question-and-answer session based on your favourite soap opera, TV series or book; if you prefer, you can base your answers on your own experiences.

You will need to do this with a partner, and you will each play the part of the interviewer and the interviewee.

Step 1
Select two different relationships to answer questions about. These should include one personal and one professional relationship, each between two individuals. Make sure you choose relationships about which you have plenty of information.

Step 2

Make notes so that you have information ready to answer the questions. The interviewer should make notes of your answers, or alternatively the interview could be recorded or videoed. The questions you need to answer are:

1   Are the relationships you have chosen real or from TV or fiction?
2   What are the two relationships you have chosen?
3   Which of them is a personal relationship and which is a professional relationship?
4   How do you know?
5   Does the personal relationship work well?
6   Why or why not?
7   Does the professional relationship work well?
8   Why or why not?
9   What are the strengths of each of the relationships?
10 What are the weaknesses?
11 What could be done to improve the weak areas of the relationships?
12 Would you like to be in either of the relationships you have chosen?
13 Why or why not?
14 How would each relationship be different if you were one of those people?

Step 3

Swap roles so that both partners have the chance to ask and answer questions.

Step 4

Give each other feedback on how well the questions were answered and how carefully the responses were listened to.

Maintain and produce records and reports

Regardless of the setting you work in, you are likely to have to keep records of the work you do. Often, completing records can feel like a chore, and something to be done in the quickest possible way. Knowing why you are completing records and what they are to be used for can often help by making the whole exercise seem more purposeful.

Broadly, records are likely to be used for a range of purposes:

▶ passing on information about the service user to others who will provide care when you are off duty
▶ passing on information to others who will meet different care needs
▶ recording statistical information for your own organisation – this will help to monitor and review present provision and to plan future services
▶ recording statistical information for national organisations – this is used to plan budgets and policies for future services
▶ providing information at the request of a court or regulatory authority
▶ providing an accurate legal record of the care provided to an individual service user. This record can be accessed by the service user and can be used in any legal dispute concerning care.

Every record you complete will have a specific use. It may sometimes feel as if organisations have forms for the sake of it, but they will all have a purpose. Make sure that you ask your supervisor about all the records you keep and what they will be used for.

Make sure it makes sense

No matter how carefully records are stored and filed, they are of no use if they cannot be understood, either because the person recording them wrote in such a way that they cannot be read – there are many millions of illegible medical case notes! – or because they are written in such a way that the meaning is not clear. Records should be clear, accurate and to the point.

Remember, you are responsible for what you write, so make sure that you can justify it and that you are accurately recording what you have seen or heard for yourself. If you want to record information which you have heard from someone else, then make sure you state clearly where the information came from.

The kind of information that you may record to pass on within your own organisation may well be different from the types of record that you would keep if you were going to send that information to another agency or if it was going into somebody else's filing system.

Sally
     Mary Johnson

Please could you make sure that you check on Mrs Johnson several times during the next shift. Nothing I can put my finger on, nothing that could go on the handover record, but she just doesn't seem herself. Please keep an eye on her.
See you tomorrow.
Sue

An informal note like the one above is often used to pass on information which is not appropriate for a formal file or record sheet, but is nevertheless important for a colleague to take note of. This is different from information which has to go outside the organisation – it would need to be formally written, and word processed using a more structured format.

Medical records

One of the very common means of transmitting information and keeping records in health and care is an observation chart recording temperature and blood pressure, like the one on page 77.

This is done in a very simple way on a graph so it is easy to see at a glance if there are any problems. The purpose of this record is to monitor a person's physical condition so that everybody who is caring for him or her is able to check on the person's well-being.

If you were to put a written record into someone's case notes or to write a report for another agency or another professional, it is unlikely that you would include the actual charts. It is far more likely that you would include a comment or an interpretation of the information on the charts similar to the one below.

Mrs J has shown no significant abnormalities in terms of raised temperature or blood pressure for the past week. It would seem to indicate her infection has now cleared up and her temperature has returned to normal after the very high levels of ten days ago.

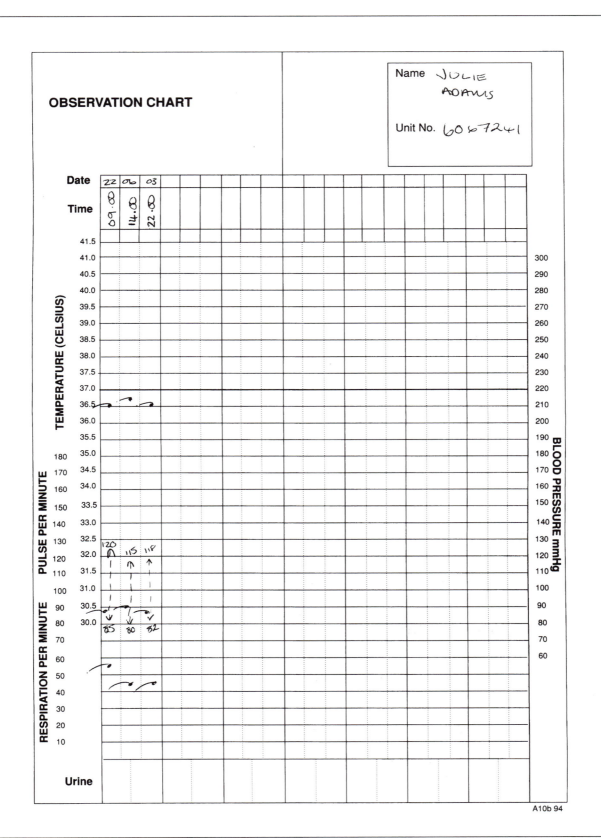

An observation chart.

Other types of record

Information which is likely to be used in making decisions about a service user is very important. It may concern a child or older person who has been the subject of a protection conference, or a young person who has been in trouble with the law and is the subject of a report for the courts, or someone with mental health problems where a background report is being provided to assist in decisions about how to best treat him or her.

Where such records are being kept for the purpose of assisting with decision-making, it is important that reports are not written in such a way that people have to read through vast amounts of material before finding the key points. It may be necessary to include a significant amount of information in order to make sure that all of the background is there, but a summary at the beginning or the end that covers the main points is always useful for a reader in a hurry.

Check it out

Find out how many different types of record are kept in your workplace. There may be reports, charts, notes, index cards ... these are just a start. Check how many there are and note what each is used for.

How to record information

If you think about the purpose for which the information is to be used, this should help you to decide on the best way to record it. There would be little point in going to the trouble of typing out a piece of information that you were simply going to pass over to a colleague on the next shift. Alternatively, if you were writing something which was to go into somebody's case notes or case file and be permanently recorded, then you would need to make sure that the information is likely to be of use to colleagues, or others who may need to have access to the file.

Check it out

Find out if your organisation has a policy about record-keeping and about where different types of information should be recorded and kept. Check whether there are clear guidelines on what should be handwritten and information that needs to be word processed.

You must make sure that you follow the guidelines and provide information in the format that your organisation needs. If you are unsure about how you should produce particular kinds of records, ask your supervisor or manager.

Keys to good practice

There are certain golden rules which are likely to be included in any organisation's policy about keeping records and recording information:

✔ All information needs to be clear.

✔ It needs to be legible (particularly if you are hand-writing it). There is nothing more useless than a piece of information in a record file which cannot be read because somebody's handwriting is poor.

✔ It should be to the point, not ramble or contain far more words than necessary.

✔ Any record should cover the important points clearly and logically.

Information policies

The **Data Protection Act 1998** provides basic rules for managing access to personal data held about any individual. It covers all types of records, not only those held on computer. The principles of data protection are set out on page 34.

The Act protects all personal information and restricts the purposes for which it can be used. It also gives people the right to know what is being held about them and to change any information that is incorrect. The information held about anybody on a computer record or database can only be used for the purpose for which it was collected.

The **Access to Medical Records Act 1988** ensures an individual has access to his or her own records but that these are not available to anyone else unless the individual gives permission.

Outcome activity 2.3

Your task in this activity is to produce a report, just as you would when working in a care setting. Even though you may not produce computer-based records at work, you should word process your work for this activity so that it is easier to share with your group. Work alone on your reports, but share and discuss your results in a group.

Step 1
Read the following scenario carefully:

You are working in Jasmine House, a 38-bed residential facility for older people. You work on the late shift, coming into work at 2 pm and leaving at 9.30 pm. Mrs J, an older service user, has been very agitated throughout your shift. She has kept asking to go home and has tried to leave several times. She has gone out of the front door on one occasion and you have managed to persuade her to come in from the garden.

Mrs J is quite mobile with the aid of a walking frame but her eyesight is poor. Otherwise she is well and, until this latest episode, had seemed settled and happy. She has a daughter who comes to visit several times each week.

Step 2
Write a report about Mrs J for the records, and to hand over to the next shift.

Step 3
Write a report for a review meeting which your supervisor has arranged in order to discuss this episode and concerns about Mrs J's current condition.

Step 4
Write a note to be given to Mrs J's daughter when she comes in the next day to let her know about what has happened with her mother.

Step 5
Compare the different records written by members of your group and see what you can learn from each other. Give and receive feedback about the records.

The maintenance of a safe and secure working environment

Every workplace is governed by regulations and legislation to protect the health and safety of those who work in it, and those who receive a service there. Each person who works in a care setting shares part of the responsibility for maintaining the workplace in a healthy, safe and secure way. The risks in a care setting are many. Of course, there are risks such as fire which apply in every workplace; but particular risks in a care setting include the moving and handling of service users, the disposal of clinical waste, and the maintenance of hygienic conditions.

This unit will give you the opportunity to learn about the regulations, guidelines and your role in contributing to a safe, clean and healthy environment.

Outcome 1: Maintain the safety and security of the working environment

What is safety?

It sounds very simple and straightforward: make sure that the place in which you work is safe and secure. However, when you start to think about it – safe for whom? From whom? Safe from tripping over things? Or safe from hazardous fumes? Safe from infection? Safe from intruders? Safe from work-related injuries? You can begin to see that this is a wide and complex subject.

You share responsibility with your employer for the safety of all the people in your care. There are many hazards which can cause injury to people, even more so if they are old, ill or disabled. This unit will explore many of the hazards, but one of the most drastic and frightening risks is fire. Knowing how to react and the correct steps to take can make the difference between survival and tragedy.

Reducing the risk of fire

Fires can be caused in many ways. It is important that you are aware of the possible risks in all areas of your work, and that you know the best ways to reduce the risk of a fire starting.

Type of risk	Action to take
Discarded or dropped cigarette	Discourage or ban smoking as far as possible Empty all ashtrays regularly Use covered ashtrays Provide sand buckets to extinguish lit smoking materials Give repeated warnings about the dangers of smoking in bed or late at night
Electrical fault	Check all electrical equipment regularly for signs of wear or damage Report wear or damage immediately for repair or replacement
Cooking fires	Never leave oil or fat unattended while heating Use alarms as a reminder to check cooking in the oven
Flammable materials	Ensure rubbish such as paper, cardboard, wood, etc. is removed and disposed of safely
Naked flames	Never leave candles or other naked flames unattended
Matches, cigarette lighters	Ensure that they are kept safely away from children or vulnerable people who may not recognise the risk.

Of course, it is always easier to check for fire risks in public areas where you have easy access. However, you will need to use sensitivity to check an individual's private space such as a bedroom. You should always seek the permission of the individual before coming into his or her room. You can check for visible risks such as candles, etc. while performing other tasks.

Fire risks in a service user's own home are rather different. Here, you can only point out the risks and make suggestions as to the best way to reduce them.

Fire safety

Your workplace will have procedures which must be followed in the case of an emergency. All workplaces must display information about what action to take in case of fire. The fire procedure is likely to be similar to the one shown below.

Fire Safety Procedure

1 Raise the alarm.

2 Inform telephonist or dial 999.

3 Ensure that everyone is safe and out of the danger area.

4 If it is safe to do so, attack fire with correct extinguisher.

5 Go to fire assembly point (this will be stated on the fire procedure notice).

6 Do not return to the building for any reason.

▶ Make sure that you know where the fire extinguishers or fire blankets are in your workplace, and where the fire exits are.

▶ Your employer will have installed fire doors to comply with regulations – *never* prop them open.

▶ Your employer should provide fire lectures each year. You must attend and make sure that you are up-to-date with the procedures to be followed.

The Fire Precautions (Workplace) (Amendment) Regulations 1999 require that all workplaces should be inspected by the fire authority to check means of escape, firefighting equipment and warnings, and that a fire certificate must be issued. A breach of fire regulations could lead to prosecution of the employer, the responsible manager, or other staff members.

Fire extinguishers

There are specific fire extinguishers for fighting different types of fire. It is important that you know this. You do not have to memorise them as each one has clear instructions on it, but you do need to be aware that there are different types and make sure that you read the instructions before use.

DID YOU KNOW?

All new fire extinguishers are red. Each one has its purpose written on it. Each one also has a patch of the colour previously used for that type of extinguisher.

Extinguisher type and colour	Use for	Danger points	How to use	How it works
Red Water	Wood, cloth, paper, plastics, coal, etc. Fires involving solids.	Do **not** use on burning fat or oil, or on electrical appliances.	Point the jet at the base of the flames and keep it moving across the area of the fire. Ensure that all areas of the fire are out.	Mainly by cooling burning material.
Blue Multi-purpose dry powder	Wood, cloth, paper, plastics, coal etc. Fires involving solids. Liquids such as grease, fats, oil, paint, petrol, etc. but **not** on chip or fat pan fires.	Safe on live electrical equipment, although the fire may re-ignite because this type of extinguisher does not cool the fire very well. Do **not** use on chip or fat pan fires.	Point the jet or discharge horn at the base of the flames and, with a rapid sweeping motion, drive the fire towards the far edge until all the flames are out.	Knocks down flames and, on burning solids, melts to form a skin smothering the fire. Provides some cooling effect.
Blue Standard dry powder	Liquids such as grease, fats, oil, paint, petrol etc. but **not** on chip or fat pan fires.	Safe on live electrical equipment, although does not penetrate the spaces in equipment easily and the fire may re-ignite. This type of extinguisher does not cool the fire very well. Do **not** use on chip or fat pan fires.	Point the jet or discharge horn at the base of the flames and, with a rapid sweeping motion, drive the fire towards the far edge until all the flames are out.	Knocks down flames.
Cream AFFF (Aqueous film-forming foam) (multi-purpose)	Wood, cloth, paper, plastics, coal, etc. Fires involving solids. Liquids such as grease, fats, oil, paint, petrol, etc. but **not** on chip or fat pan fires.	Do **not** use on chip or fat pan fires.	For fires involving solids, point the jet at the base of the flames and keep it moving across the area of the fire. Ensure that all areas of the fire are out. For fires involving liquids, do not aim the jet straight into the liquid. Where the liquid on fire is in a container, point the jet at the inside edge of the container or on a nearby surface above the burning liquid. Allow the foam to build up and flow across the liquid.	Forms a fire-extinguishing film on the surface of a burning liquid. Has a cooling action with a wider extinguishing application than water on solid combustible materials.

Extinguisher type and colour	Use for	Danger points	How to use	How it works
Cream Foam	Limited number of liquid fires.	Do **not** use on chip or fat pan fires. Check manufacturer's instructions for suitability of use on other fires involving liquids.	Do not aim jet straight into the liquid. Where the liquid on fire is in a container, point the jet at the inside edge of the container or on a nearby surface above the burning liquid. Allow the foam to build up and flow across the liquid.	
Black Carbon dioxide CO_2	Liquids such as grease, fats, oil, paint, petrol, etc. but **not** on chip or fat pan fires.	Do **not** use on chip or fat pan fires. This type of extinguisher does not cool the fire very well. Fumes from CO_2 extinguishers can be harmful if used in confined spaces: ventilate the area as soon as the fire has been controlled.	Direct the discharge horn at the base of the flames and keep the jet moving across the area of the fire.	Vaporising liquid gas smothers the flames by displacing oxygen in the air.
Fire blanket	Fires involving both solids and liquids. Particularly good for small fires in clothing and for chip and fat pan fires, provided the blanket **completely** covers the fire.	If the blanket does not completely cover the fire, it will not be extinguished.	Place carefully over the fire. Keep your hands shielded from the fire. Take care not to waft the fire towards you.	Smothers the fire.

Evacuating buildings

You may be involved in evacuating buildings if there is a fire, or for other reasons, such as:

- a bomb scare
- the building has become structurally unsafe
- an explosion
- a leak of dangerous chemicals or fumes.

The evacuation procedure you need to follow will be laid down by your workplace. The information will be the same whatever the emergency is: the same exits will be used and the same assembly point. It is likely to be along the following lines:

- Stay calm, do not shout or run.
- Do not allow others to run.
- Organise people quickly and firmly without panic.
- Direct those who can move themselves and assist those who cannot.
- Use wheelchairs to move people quickly.
- Move the bed with the person in, if necessary.

Your workplace must arrange regular fire or evacuation drills and testing of the alarm equipment. The results of the drills will be recorded so that your employer has a record of how long it took to clear the buildings and a report of how effective the evacuation was.

How to maintain security

Most workplaces where care is provided are not under lock and key. This is part of creating an environment where people have choice and their rights are respected. However, they also have a right to be secure. Security in a care environment is about:

- security against intruders
- security in respect of people's privacy and decisions about unwanted visitors
- security against being abused
- security of property.

Security against intruders

If you work for a large organisation, such as an NHS trust, it may be that all employees are easily identifiable by identity badges with photographs. Some of

these even contain a microchip which allows the card to be 'swiped' to gain access to secure parts of the building. This makes it easier to identify people who do not have a right to be on the premises.

Less sophisticated systems in smaller workplaces may use a keypad with a code number known only to staff and those who are legitimately on the premises. It is often difficult to maintain security with such systems, as codes are forgotten or become widely known. In order to maintain security, it is necessary to change the codes regularly, and to make sure everyone is aware.

Another possible system for a smaller workplace is to issue visitors' badges to people who have reasons to be there. Some workplaces still operate with keys, although the days of staff walking about with large bunches of keys attached to a belt are fast disappearing. If mechanical keys are used, there will be a list of named keyholders and there is likely to be a system of handover of keys at shift change. However, each workplace will have its own system and you will need to be sure that you understand the security system that operates in your workplace.

Keys to good practice

✔ Be aware of everyone you come across. Get into the habit of noticing people and thinking, 'Do I know that person?'
✔ Challenge anyone you do not recognise.
✔ The challenge should be polite. 'Can I help you?' is usually enough to find out if a visitor has a reason to be on the premises.

If a person says that he or she is there to see someone:

✔ Don't give directions – escort him or her.
✔ If the person is a genuine visitor, he or she will be grateful. If not, he or she will disappear pretty quickly!

The more dependent individuals are, the greater the risk. If you work with babies, high-dependency or unconscious patients, people with a severe learning disability or multiple disabilities, or people who are very confused, you will have to be extremely vigilant in protecting them from criminals.

Workplaces where most or all service users are in individual rooms can also be difficult to make secure as it is not always possible to check every room if service users choose to close the door. A routine check can be very time-consuming and can affect service users' rights to privacy and dignity.

Communal areas are easier to check, but they can present their own problems; it can be difficult to be sure who is a legitimate visitor and who should not be there. Giving all visitors badges may be acceptable in a large institution or an office block, but it is not compatible with creating a comfortable and relaxed atmosphere in a residential setting. Extra care must be taken to check that you know all the people in a communal area. If you are not sure, ask. It is better to risk offending someone by asking 'Can I help you?' or 'Are you waiting for someone?' than to leave an intruder unchallenged.

REMEMBER

If you find an intruder on the premises, don't tackle him or her – raise the alarm.

Protecting people at home

If very dependent individuals are living in their own homes, the risks are far greater. You must try to impress on them the importance of finding out who people are before letting them in. If they are able to use it, the 'password' scheme for callers from the utilities (water, gas and electricity companies) is helpful. Information record cards like those provided by the 'Safe as Houses' scheme can be invaluable in providing basic information to anyone who is involved in helping in an emergency.

REMEMBER

▶ Every time you visit, you may have to explain again what the individual should do when someone knocks on the door.
▶ Give the individual a card with simple instructions.
▶ Obtain agreement to speak to the local 'homewatch' scheme and ask that a special eye is kept on visitors.
▶ Speak to the local police and make them aware that a vulnerable individual is living alone in the house.

Security of property

Property and valuables belonging to individuals in care settings should be safeguarded. It is likely that your employer will have a property book in which records of all valuables and personal possessions are entered.

There may be particular policies within your organisation, but as a general rule you are likely to need to:

▶ make a record of all possessions on admission
▶ record valuable items separately
▶ describe items of jewellery by their colour, for example 'yellow metal', not 'gold'
▶ ensure that individuals sign for any valuables they are keeping, and that they understand that they are liable for their loss
▶ inform your manager if an individual is keeping valuables or a significant amount of money.

Check it out

Find out where the property book is in your workplace, and how it is filled in. Check who has the responsibility to complete it. If you are likely to have to use the book at any time, make sure you know exactly what your role is. Do you have to enter the property in the book, then give it to someone else to deal with the valuables? Do you have to make sure the valuables are safe? Do you have to give the individual a copy of the entry in the book? Ask the questions in advance – don't leave it until you have to do it.

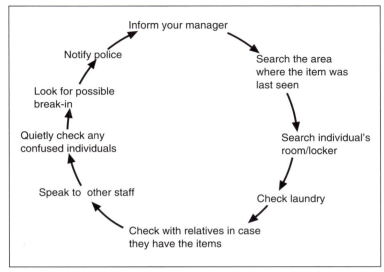

Action stages when property goes missing.

It is always difficult when items go missing in a care setting, particularly if they are valuable. It is important that you check all possibilities before calling the police.

Restricting access

People also have a right to choose who they see. This can often be a difficult area to deal with. If there are relatives or friends who wish to visit and an individual does not want to see them, you may have to make this clear. It is difficult to do, but you can only be effective if you are clear and assertive. You should not make excuses or invent reasons why visitors cannot see the person concerned. You could say something like: 'I'm sorry, Mr P has told us that he does not want to see you. I understand that this may be upsetting, but it is his choice. If he does change his mind we will contact you. Would you like to leave your phone number?'

Do not allow yourself to be drawn into passing on messages or attempting to persuade – that is not your role. Your job is to respect the wishes of the person you are caring for. If you are asked to intervene or to pass on a message, you must refuse politely but firmly: 'I'm sorry, that is not something I can do. If your uncle does decide he wants to see you, I will let you know right away. I will tell him you have visited, but I can't do anything else.'

There may also be occasions when access is restricted for other reasons; possibly because someone is seriously ill and there are medical reasons for limiting access, or because of a legal restriction such as a court order. In either case, it should be clearly recorded on the service user's record and your supervisor will advise you about the restrictions.

Check it out

You need a colleague or friend to try this. One of you should play the role of a person who has come to visit, and the other the care worker who has to tell him or her that the friend or relative will not agree to the visit. Try using different scenarios – the visitor becomes angry, upset, aggressive, and so on. Try at least three different scenarios each. By the time you have practised a few times, you may feel better equipped to deal with the situation when it happens in reality.

If you cannot find anyone to work with you, it is possible to do a similar exercise by imagining three or four different scenarios and then writing down the words you would say in each of the situations.

The legal framework

The settings in which you provide care are generally covered by the Health and Safety at Work Act 1974 (HASAWA). This Act has been updated and supplemented by many sets of regulations and guidelines, which extend it, support it or explain it.

The effect of the laws

There are many regulations, laws and guidelines dealing with health and safety. You do not need to know the detail, but you do need to know where your responsibilities begin and end.

The laws place certain responsibilities on both employers and employees. For example, it is up to the employer to provide a safe place in which to work, but the employee also has to show reasonable care for his or her own safety.

Employers have to:

▶ provide a safe workplace
▶ ensure that there is safe access to and from the workplace
▶ provide information on health and safety
▶ provide health and safety training
▶ undertake risk assessment for all hazards.

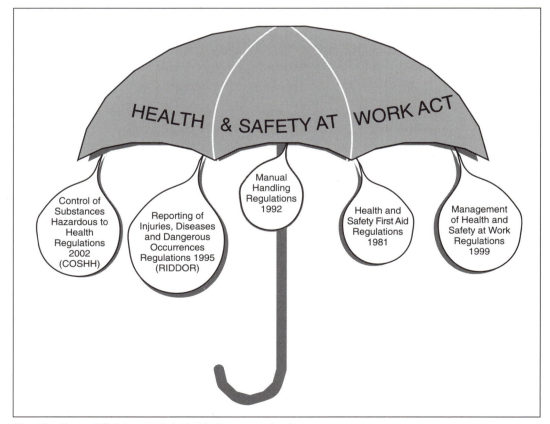

The Health and Safety at Work Act is like an umbrella.

Workers must:

- take reasonable care for their own safety and that of others
- co-operate with the employer in respect of health and safety matters
- not intentionally damage any health and safety equipment or materials provided by the employer.

Both the employee and employer are jointly responsible for safeguarding the health and safety of anyone using the premises. Any hazards you come across should be reported to your supervisor immediately so that steps can be taken promptly. Each workplace will have its own reporting system for hazards identified by staff. This can be as simple as telling a senior member of staff, or it may involve recording it in some way so that it can be passed on. Make sure that you know the procedure for reporting hazards in your workplace.

Each workplace where there are five or more workers must have a written statement of its health and safety policy. The policy must include:

- a statement of intention to provide a safe workplace
- the name of the person responsible for implementing the policy
- the names of any other individuals responsible for particular health and safety hazards
- a list of identified health and safety hazards and the procedures to be followed in relation to them
- procedures for recording accidents at work
- details for evacuation of the premises.

Check it out

Find out where the health and safety policy is for your workplace and make sure you read it.

Outcome activity 3.1

This activity should be based on your own workplace if possible. If not, you could use any other suitable establishment. You could work on your own, or in a small group.

Step 1
Draw a plan to scale of your workplace showing at least three rooms, the entrance and at least one emergency escape route other than the main entrance. Show the reception area if there is one, all the doorways and windows. If you have access to a suitable computer program, and the necessary skills, use IT to produce your plan.

Step 2
Mark on your plan all the fire extinguishers and/or fire blankets available.

Mark any security checking systems on doors or in the reception area.

Clearly show emergency escape routes.

Identify any potential hazards.

Step 3

Make notes, either on the plan or using a key to the plan, about:

▶ the types of fire extinguisher in each location and why they are appropriate
▶ how the security checking systems operate and why they are needed
▶ how an emergency evacuation would be undertaken
▶ what the hazards are and how they should be assessed.

Step 4

Present your findings and your plan to your tutor.

Risk assessment

The Management of Health and Safety at Work Regulations 1999 states that employers have to assess any risks which are associated with the workplace and

work activities. This means *all* activities, from walking on wet floors to dealing with violence. Having carried out a risk assessment, the employer must then apply **risk control measures**. This means that actions must be taken to reduce the risks. For example, alarm buzzers may need to be installed or extra staff employed, as well as steps like providing extra training for staff or written guidelines on how to deal with a particular hazard.

Risks in someone's home

Of course, the situation is somewhat different if you work in an individual's own home. Your employer can still carry out risk assessments and put risk control measures in place, such as a procedure for working in twos in a situation where there is a risk of violence. What cannot be done is to remove environmental hazards such as trailing electrical flexes, rugs with curled up edges, worn patches on stair carpets or old equipment. All you can do is to advise the person whose home it is of the risks, and suggest how things could be improved. You also need to take care!

REMEMBER

▶ It may be your workplace, but it is the person's home. If you work in an individual's home or long-term residential setting, you have to balance the need for safety with the rights of people to have their living space the way they want it.

▶ Both you and the individuals receiving care are entitled to expect a safe place in which to live and work, but remember their rights to choose how they want to live.

Working safely

It is important that you develop an awareness of health and safety risks and that you are always aware of any risks in any situation you are in. If you get into the habit of making a mental checklist, you will find that it helps. The checklist will vary from one workplace to another, but could look like the one on the next page.

Checklist for a safe work environment

Hazards	Check
Environment	
Floors	Are they dry?
Carpets and rugs	Are they worn or curled at the edges?
Doorways and corridors	Are they clear of obstacles?
Electrical flexes	Are they trailing?
Equipment	
Beds	Are the brakes on? Are they high enough?
Electrical or gas appliances	Are they worn? Have they been safety checked?
Lifting equipment	Is it worn or damaged?
Mobility aids	Are they worn or damaged?
Substances such as cleaning fluids	Are they correctly labelled?
Containers	Are they leaking or damaged?
Waste disposal equipment	Is it faulty?
People	
Visitors to the building	Should they be there?
Handling procedures	Have they been assessed for risk?
Intruders	Have police been called?
Violent and aggressive behaviour	Has it been dealt with?

What you wear in the workplace has an important bearing on health and safety. What problems can you see in this picture?

What you wear

You may not think that what you wear has much bearing on health and safety, but it is important. Even if your employer supplies, or insists on you wearing, a uniform, there are still other aspects to the safety of your work outfit.

There may be restrictions on wearing jewellery or carrying things in your pocket which could cause injury. This can also pose a risk to you – you could be stabbed in the chest by a pair of scissors or ball-point pen!

Many workplaces do not allow the wearing of rings with stones. Not only is this a possible source of infection, but they can also scratch people or tear protective gloves.

High-heeled or poorly supporting shoes are a risk to you in terms of foot injuries and very sore feet! They also present a risk to individuals you are helping, because if you overbalance or stumble, so will they.

Simple precautions can often be the most effective in reducing the risk. Always look for the risk and take steps to reduce it.

THINK RISK → ASSESS → REDUCE → AVOID

Keeping food safe

Maintaining the safety and hygiene of food provided for service users is an essential part of a safe and healthy environment. If you are preparing areas or equipment for people who are about to eat or drink, it is important that you follow basic hygiene procedures. It is also important that you know how to store and prepare food safely. Ensuring that food is not contaminated by bacteria is a matter which raises many questions, for instance:

You need to learn basic hygiene procedures if you are involved in preparing or serving food.

Q What personal precautions do I need to take to ensure that I am hygienic?

A You must make sure that if you have long hair, it is tied back or covered. You should ensure that your nails are short and clean and that you are not wearing any jewellery in which food could become trapped, such as rings with stones, etc. You must ensure that you wash your hands thoroughly at each stage of food preparation and between handling raw food and cooked food, or raw meat and food which will not be cooked. You must always wash your hands after going to the toilet. Do not touch your nose during food handling or preparation.

Q What should I do if I have a cut or sore on my hands?

A You must wear a special blue adhesive plaster dressing. This is because no food is blue, and if the plaster should come off during food preparation it will be easy to locate.

Q How does food become contaminated?

A Food is contaminated by bacteria which infect food directly, especially if it is not heated or chilled properly, or by cross-contamination, which is where bacteria are spread by somebody preparing food with unclean hands or equipment.

Q What are the main bacteria that cause contamination of food?

A Campylobacter, salmonella and e.coli are types of bacteria that can cause serious food poisoning in people who are old, ill or in young children. **Campylobacter** is the most common cause of food poisoning in the UK. It can be found in undercooked chicken and red meat, and also in untreated milk and water. **Salmonella** is the second most common cause of food poisoning in the UK. Salmonella survives when refrigerated but is killed by cooking or pasteurising. It can be found in raw eggs or raw chicken and meat. Escherichia coli (**E.coli**) can cause severe illness. It is found in raw and undercooked meat (especially burgers and pies), unpasteurised milk and dairy products, and raw vegetables.

Q How can infection and cross-contamination be avoided?

A Raw meat is a source of bacteria and you should be sure to use separate utensils and chopping boards or areas for raw food and for cooked food. For example, do not chop the raw chicken breasts and then chop the lettuce for the accompanying salad on the same chopping board or with the same knife. This may give everybody who eats your salad a nasty dose of salmonella. You should keep separate chopping boards for meat and vegetables, and ensure that you use different knives. Remember to change knives and wash your hands between preparing different types of food.

Q Does it matter whether food is to be cooked or not?

A It is possible to kill bacteria by cooking food. But be careful with foods which are not cooked, such as salads or mayonnaise, that you are not using contaminated utensils to prepare them.

Q How hot does food have to be to kill bacteria?

A A core temperature of 75°C will kill bacteria. Hot food should be heated or re-heated to at least this temperature.

Q How cold does food have to be to kill bacteria?

A By law, food should be stored at below 8°C. However, good practice dictates that food is stored below 5°C to be free from any risk of contamination with bacteria. A fridge with the door left open rapidly warms up to above 5°C or 8°C, and food can deteriorate quite quickly and become dangerous. Food in a fridge where the door has been left open or where the power has been cut off should be discarded.

Q What other safety steps should I take with the fridge?

A When you arrange food in a fridge, you should be sure that you put any raw meat on the bottom shelf to stop any moisture or blood dripping from the meat onto any of the foods stored below – moisture or blood from uncooked meat could be infected with bacteria. Fridges should be kept scrupulously

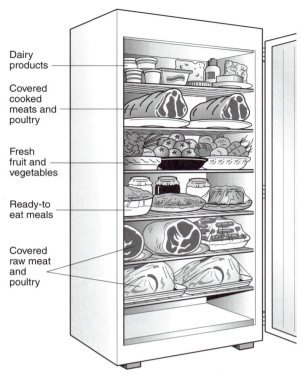

Dairy products

Covered cooked meats and poultry

Fresh fruit and vegetables

Ready-to eat meals

Covered raw meat and poultry

Correct storage of food in a fridge.

clean and should be regularly washed out with an anti-bacterial solution. Do not allow particles of food to build up on the inside of the fridge. It is also important that the fridge does not become 'iced up' as this will make the motor work harder in order to keep it cold and could result in a warming of the fridge.

Q   What about 'best before' dates?

A   These are provided by the manufacturers to ensure that food is not kept by retailers beyond a date when it is safe to eat. Many manufacturers now include instructions about how soon the food should be consumed after purchase. These should be followed carefully. As a general rule, unless the manufacturer indicates otherwise, you should consume food by its 'best before' date in order to ensure that it has not begun to deteriorate.

How to maintain personal safety

There is always an element of risk in working with people. There is little doubt that there is an increase in the level of personal abuse suffered by workers in the health and care services. There is also the element of personal risk encountered by workers who visit people in the community, and have to deal with homes in poor states of repair and an assortment of domestic animals!

However, there are some steps which you can take to assist with safety.

Keys to good practice

✔ If you work alone in the community, always leave details of where you are going and what time you expect to return. This is important in case of accidents or other emergencies, so that you can be found.
✔ Carry a personal alarm, and use it if necessary.
✔ Ask your employer to provide training in techniques to combat aggression and violence. It is foolish and potentially dangerous to go into risky situations without any training.
✔ Try to defuse potentially aggressive situations by being as calm as possible and by talking quietly and reasonably. But if this is not effective, leave.
✔ If you work in a residential or hospital setting, raise the alarm if you find you are in a threatening situation.
✔ Do not tackle aggressors, whoever they are – raise the alarm.
✔ Use an alarm or panic button if you have it. Otherwise shout – very loudly.

Missing persons

If a service user goes missing, your workplace will have set procedures to follow. If you work in a residential or supported living setting, the response is likely to involve the following steps.

▶ Check all possibilities inside the building: bedrooms, bathrooms, laundry, kitchen, outbuildings, etc.
▶ If the service user is someone who regularly wanders, it may be usual to check places where he or she has been found previously. It is quite common for older people to return to a previous home or an area where they lived as a child.
▶ Wait a certain amount of time to see if the service user returns. The amount of time is likely to depend on the vulnerability of the service user.
▶ If the missing service user is the subject of a compulsory admission or a court order, inform the police.
▶ Contact police with a description of the missing service user and details of the clothes he or she was wearing.
▶ Contact local Social Services departments with the same information.
▶ Contact relatives to advise them and to ask them to check any known possibilities to help locate the service user.

This procedure is likely to be the responsibility of the most senior person on duty at the time.

Making waste safe

As part of providing a safe working environment, employers have to put procedures in place to deal with waste materials and spillages. There are various types of waste, which must be dealt with in particular ways. These are summarised in the table below.

Type of waste	Method of disposal
Clinical waste – used dressings	Yellow bags, clearly labelled with contents and location. This waste is incinerated.
Needles, syringes, cannulas ('sharps')	Yellow sharps box. Never put sharps into anything other than a hard plastic box. This is sealed and incinerated.
Body fluids and waste – urine, vomit, blood, sputum, faeces	Cleared and flushed down sluice drain. Area to be cleaned and disinfected.
Soiled linen	Red bags, direct into laundry, bags disintegrate in wash. If handled, gloves must be worn.
Recyclable instruments and equipment	Blue bags, to be returned to the Central Sterilisation Services Department (CSSD) for recycling and sterilising.

Check it out

Look carefully around your workplace. Try to identify six potential hazards, or risky activities. When you have chosen them, check through the Health and Safety Manual and find the risk control measures and provisions made for each of them. If you believe that you have noticed a potential risk which your employer has not covered, you should discuss it with your manager or supervisor immediately.

Controlling infection

The very nature of work in a care setting means that great care must be taken to control the spread of infection. You will come into contact with a number of people during your working day – an ideal opportunity for infection to spread. Infection which spreads from one person to another is called 'cross-infection'. If you work in the community, cross-infection is difficult to control. However, if you work in a residential or hospital setting, infection control is essential. There are various steps which you can take in terms of the way you carry out your work (wherever you work), which can help to prevent the spread of infection.

You do not know what viruses or bacteria may be present in any individual, so it is important that you take precautions when dealing with everyone. The precautions are called 'universal precautions' precisely because you need to take them with everyone you deal with.

Wear gloves

When	Why	How
Any occasion when you will have contact with body fluids (including body waste, blood, mucus, sputum, sweat or vomit), or when you have any contact with anyone with a rash, pressure sore, wound, bleeding or any broken skin.	Because gloves act as a protective barrier against infection.	Check gloves before putting them on. Never use gloves with holes or tears. Check that they are not cracked or faded. Pull gloves on, making sure that they fit properly. If you are wearing a gown, pull them over the cuffs. Take them off by

You must also wear gloves when you clear up spills of blood or body fluids or have to deal with soiled linen or dressings.		pulling from the cuff – this turns the glove inside out. Pull off the second glove while holding the first so that the two gloves are folded together inside out. Dispose of them in the correct waste disposal container and wash your hands.

Wash your hands

When	Why	How
Before and after carrying out any procedure which has involved contact with an individual, or with any body fluids, soiled linen or clinical waste. You must wash your hands even though you have worn gloves. You must also wash your hands before you start and after you finish your shift, before and after eating, after using the toilet and after coughing, sneezing or blowing your nose.	Because hands are a major route to spreading infection. When tests have been carried out on people's hands, an enormous number of bacteria have been found.	In running water, in a basin deep enough to hold the splashes and with either foot pedals or elbow bars rather than taps, because you can re-infect your hands from still water in a basin, or from touching taps with your hands once they have been washed. Use the soaps and disinfectants supplied. Make sure that you wash thoroughly, including between your fingers.

Wear protective clothing

When	Why	How
You should always wear a gown or plastic apron for any procedure which involves bodily contact or is likely to deal with body waste or fluids. An apron is preferable, unless it is likely to be very messy, as gowns can be a little frightening.	Because it will reduce the spread of infection by preventing infection getting on your clothes and spreading to the next person you come into contact with.	The plastic apron should be disposable and thrown away at the end of each procedure. You should use a new apron for each individual you come into contact with.

Tie up hair

Why
Because if it hangs over your face, it is more likely to come into contact with the individual you are working with and could spread infection. It could also become entangled in equipment and cause a serious injury.

Clean equipment

Why	How
Because infection can spread from one person to another on instruments, linen and equipment just as easily as on hands or hair.	By washing large items like trolleys with antiseptic solution. Small instruments must be sterilised. Do not shake soiled linen or dump it on the floor. Keep it held away from you. Place linen in proper bags or hampers for laundering.

Deal with waste

Why	How
Because it can then be processed correctly, and the risk to others working further along the line in the disposal process is reduced as far as possible.	By placing it in the proper bags. Make sure that you know the system in your workplace. It is usually: • clinical waste – yellow • soiled linen – red • recyclable instruments and equipment – blue.

Take special precautions

Why	How
There may be occasions when you have to deal with an individual who has a particular type of infection that requires special handling. This can involve things like hepatitis, some types of food poisoning or highly infectious diseases.	Your workplace will have special procedures to follow. They may include such measures as gowning, double gloving or wearing masks. Follow the procedures strictly. They are there for your benefit and for the benefit of the other individuals you care for.

Check it out

Make notes of three ways in which infection can be spread. Then note down three effective ways to reduce the possibility of cross-infection.

Reporting problems

In your workplace, you have a responsibility to report any unsafe situation to your employer. For example, if you come across a piece of equipment – anything from a hoist to a kettle – that is unsafe or needs repair, you must report it. It is not enough to assume that someone else will notice it, or to say 'It's not up to me – that's a manager's job'. You have a share in the responsibility for making your workplace safe and secure.

However, there are some serious situations which have to reported officially, not just to your employer, and there are special procedures to be followed.

Reporting of Injuries, Diseases and Dangerous Occurrences (RIDDOR)

Reporting accidents and ill-health at work is a legal requirement. All accidents, diseases and dangerous occurrences should be reported to the Incident Contact Centre. The Contact Centre was established on 1 April 2001 as a single point of contact for all incidents in the UK. The information is important because it means that risks and causes of accidents, incidents and diseases can be identified. All notifications are passed on to either the local authority Environmental Health department, or the Health and Safety Executive, as appropriate.

Your employer needs to report:

- deaths
- major injuries (see below)
- accidents resulting in more than three days off work
- diseases
- dangerous occurrences.

Reportable major injuries and diseases

The following injuries need to be reported:

- fracture other than to fingers, thumbs or toes
- amputation
- dislocation of the shoulder, hip, knee or spine
- loss of sight (temporary or permanent)
- chemical or hot metal burn to the eye or any penetrating injury to the eye
- injury resulting from an electric shock or electrical burn leading to unconsciousness or requiring resuscitation or admittance to hospital for more than 24 hours
- any other injury which leads to hypothermia (getting too cold), heat-induced illness, or unconsciousness; requires resuscitation; or requires admittance to hospital for more than 24 hours
- unconsciousness caused by asphyxia (suffocation) or exposure to a harmful substance or biological agent
- acute illness requiring medical treatment, or leading to loss of consciousness, arising from absorption of any substance by inhalation, ingestion or through the skin
- acute illness requiring medical treatment where there is reason to believe that this resulted from exposure to a biological agent or its toxins or infected material.

Reportable diseases include:

- certain poisonings
- some skin diseases such as occupational dermatitis, skin cancer, chrome ulcer, oil folliculitis acne
- lung diseases including occupational asthma, farmer's lung, pneumoconiosis, asbestosis, mesothelioma
- infections such as: leptospirosis, hepatitis, tuberculosis, anthrax, legionellosis (Legionnaires' disease) and tetanus
- other conditions such as occupational cancer, certain musculoskeletal disorders, decompression illness and hand-arm vibration syndrome.

Dangerous occurrences

If something happens which does not result in a reportable injury, but which clearly could have done, then it may be a dangerous occurrence which must be reported immediately.

Accidents at work

If accidents or injuries occur at work, either to you or to an individual you are caring for, then the details must be recorded. For example, someone may have a fall, or slip on a wet floor. You must record the incident regardless of whether there was an injury.

Your employer should have procedures in place for making a record of accidents, either an accident book or an accident report form. This is not only required by the **RIDDOR** regulations, but also, if you work in a residential or nursing home, by the Care Standards Commission.

Make sure you know where the accident report forms or the accident book are kept, and who is responsible for recording accidents. It is likely to be your manager.

You must report any accident in which you are involved, or that you have witnessed, to your manager or supervisor.

Any medical treatment or assessment which is necessary should be arranged without delay. If an individual has been involved in an accident, you should check if there is anyone he or she would like to be contacted, perhaps a relative or friend. If the accident is serious, and you cannot consult the individual –

Date: 24.3.04   **Time:** 14.30 hrs   **Location:** Main lounge

Description of accident:
PH got out of her chair and began to walk across the lounge with the aid of her stick. She turned her head to continue the conversation she had been having with GK, and as she turned back again she appeared not to have noticed that MP's handbag had been left on the floor. PH tripped over handbag and fell heavily, banging her head on a footstool.

She was very shaken and although she said that she was not hurt, there was a large bump on her head. P appeared pale and shaky. I asked J to fetch a blanket and to call Mrs J, deputy officer in charge. Covered P with a blanket. Mrs J arrived immediately. Dr was sent for after P was examined by Mrs J.

Dr arrived after about 20 mins and said that she was bruised and shaken, but did not seem to have any injuries.

She wanted to go and lie down. She was helped to bed.

Incident was witnessed by six residents who were in the lounge at the time: GK, MP, IL, MC, CR and BQ.

Signed   Name:

-          - - - - - - - - - - - - - -

An example of an accident report.

because he or she is unconscious, for example – the next of kin should be informed as soon as possible.

Complete a report, and ensure that all witnesses to the accident also complete reports. You should include the following in any accident report (see the example on page 104):

- date, time and place of accident
- person/people involved
- circumstances and details of exactly what you saw
- anything which was said by the individuals involved
- the condition of the individual after the accident
- steps taken to summon help, time of summoning help and time when help arrived
- names of any other people who witnessed the accident
- any equipment involved in the accident.

Check it out

Your manager has asked you to design a new incident/accident report form for your workplace. She has asked you to do this because the current form does not provide enough information. The purpose of the new form is to provide sufficient information to:

- ensure the individual receives the proper medical attention

- provide information for treatment at a later date, in case of delayed reactions

- give information to any inspector who may need to see the records

- identify any gaps or need for improvements in safety procedures

- provide information about the circumstances in case of any future legal action.

Think about how you would design the new report form and what headings you would include. Use the list above as a checklist to make sure you have covered everything you need.

Safe storage of hazardous material

Safe workplaces depend on the careful use and storage of cleaning materials, and other potentially hazardous substances.

What are hazardous substances? There are many substances hazardous to health – nicotine, many drugs, even too much alcohol! The Control of Substances Hazardous to Health Regulations (COSHH), however, apply to substances which have been identified as being toxic, corrosive or irritant. This includes cleaning materials, pesticides, acids, disinfectants and bleaches, and naturally occurring substances such as blood, bacteria, etc. Workplaces may have other hazardous substances which are particular to the nature of the work carried out.

Employers must take the following steps to protect employees from hazardous substances.

▶ Find out what hazardous substances are used in the workplace and the risks these substances pose to people's health.
▶ Decide what precautions are needed before any work starts with hazardous substances.
▶ Prevent people from being exposed to hazardous substances, but where this is not reasonably practicable, control the exposure.
▶ Make sure control measures are used and maintained properly, and that safety procedures are followed.
▶ If required, monitor exposure of employees to hazardous substances.
▶ Carry out health surveillance where assessment has shown that this is necessary, or COSHH makes specific requirements.
▶ If required, prepare plans and procedures to deal with accidents, incidents and emergencies.
▶ Make sure employees are properly informed, trained and supervised.

(*Health and Safety Executive, 2002*)

COSHH (Control of Substances Hazardous to Health) file

Every workplace must have a COSHH file. This file lists all the hazardous substances used in the workplace. It should detail:

▶ where they are kept
▶ how they are labelled
▶ their effects
▶ the maximum amount of time it is safe to be exposed to them
▶ how to deal with an emergency involving one of them.

Check it out

Ask to see the COSHH file in your workplace. Make sure you read it and know which substances you use or come into contact with. Check in the file what the maximum exposure limits are. Your employer must include this information in the COSHH file.

If you have to work with hazardous substances, which may be cleaning or other materials, make sure that you take the precautions detailed in the COSHH file – this may be wearing gloves or protective goggles, or it may involve limiting the time you are exposed to the substance or only using it in certain circumstances.

The COSHH file should also give you information about how to store hazardous substances. This will involve using the correct containers as supplied by the manufacturers. All containers must have safety lids and caps, and must be correctly labelled.

Never use the container of one substance for storing another, and *never* change the labels.

These symbols, which warn you of hazardous substances, are always yellow.

The symbols above indicate hazardous substances. They are there for your safety and for the safety of those you care for. Before you use *any* substance, whether it is liquid, powder, spray, cream or aerosol, take the following simple steps:

▶ Check the container for the hazard symbol.
▶ If there is a hazard symbol, go to the COSHH file.
▶ Look up the precautions you need to take with the substance.
▶ Make sure you follow procedures, which are intended to protect you.

If you are concerned that a substance being used in your workplace is not in the COSHH file, or if you notice incorrect containers or labels being used, report it to your supervisor. Once you have informed your supervisor, it becomes his or her responsibility to act to correct the problem.

Manual handling

One of the commonest causes of accidents to care workers, and often to service users, is the process of moving people around when they need assistance.

DID YOU KNOW?

Lifting and handling individuals is the single largest cause of injuries at work in health and care settings. One in four workers take time off because of a back injury sustained at work.

The Manual Handling Operations Regulations 1993 require employers to avoid all manual handling where there is a risk of injury 'so far as it is reasonably practical'. Everyone from the European Commission to the Royal College of Nurses has issued policies and directives about avoiding lifting, but these have been the subject of legal challenge (see page 109). Make sure you check out the policies in use in your workplace and that you understand them.

There is almost no situation in which manual lifting and handling could be considered acceptable, but the views and rights of the service user being lifted must be taken into account and a balance achieved.

REMEMBER

▶ Always use lifting and handling aids.

▶ There is no such thing as a safe lift.

▶ Use the aids which your employer is obliged to provide.

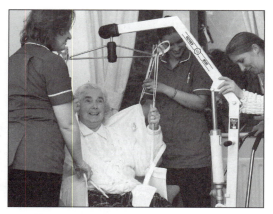

Use lifting aids and hoists whenever possible.

On the rare occasions when it is still absolutely necessary for manual lifting to be done, the employer has to make a 'risk assessment' and put procedures in place to reduce the risk of injury to the employee. This could involve ensuring that sufficient staff are available to lift or handle someone safely, which can often mean that four people are needed.

All lifting and handling should be carried out using appropriate aids and sufficient people. Manual lifting is not something to be undertaken in the normal course of events and you should use mechanical lifting aids and hoists wherever possible.

REMEMBER

Your employer has a statutory duty to install lifting equipment, but it is your responsibility to use the equipment that is there.

Use the aids which your employer is obliged to provide.

If you do have to lift, what should you do?

Encourage all individuals to help themselves – you would be surprised how much 'learned helplessness' exists. This is largely brought about by care workers who find it is quicker and easier to do things themselves rather than allowing a person to do it for himself or herself!

It is also essential that the views of the person being moved are taken into account. While you and your employer need to make sure that you are not put at risk by moving or lifting, it is also important that the person needing assistance is not caused pain, distress or humiliation. Groups representing disabled people have pointed out that blanket policies which exclude any lifting may infringe the human rights of an individual needing mobility assistance. For example, individuals may in effect be confined to bed unnecessarily and against their will by a lack of lifting assistance. A High Court judgement (A & B vs East Sussex County Council, 2003) found in favour of two disabled women who had been denied access to lifting because the local authority had a 'blanket ban' on lifting regardless of circumstances. Such a ban was deemed unlawful. It is likely that similar cases will be brought under the Human Rights Act, which gives people protection against humiliating or degrading treatment.

REMEMBER

▶ Many workers in care still lift people manually. It seems quicker and easier than going to all the trouble of using a hoist – it isn't.

▶ Manual lifting is now actively discouraged throughout the profession.

▶ Manual lifting usually presents unnecessary and unacceptable risks to the service user and to you.

▶ The wishes of the service user must be taken into account.

▶ A back injury can end your career. It's not worth the risk.

Your employer should arrange for you to attend a lifting and handling course. You must attend one each year, so that you are up-to-date with the safest possible practices.

Medication

If you are working in a nursing home or other long-term residential setting, or if you are supporting service users in their own homes, you may be involved in assisting them to take medication. This will have been prescribed by a doctor, or could be over-the-counter medicines which have been recommended. The range of medications that you may need to administer includes:

- oral medicines (those taken by mouth)
- inhaled medicines
- eye, nose and ear drops
- vaginal and rectal preparations
- topical preparations (those applied to the skin).

Prescribed medication

If a service user has a prescription for medication from a doctor, then it will be important that you obtain the medication where necessary. Your workplace may have a system for obtaining a batch of medication from a local chemist, who may operate a delivery service. If a service user has requested you to purchase a particular medicine for him or her, you should check with the care plan and the medical practitioner that it will not interfere with any prescribed medicines that he or she is taking.

Administering medication requires a hygienic technique. Always wash your hands before providing any medication, whether it is in tablet, cream, lotion, drops or pessary form.

Labelling

Where medications are prescribed for a service user, it is essential that you check each time that the medication you are administering is the correct one for that service user. There should be a label, clearly marked with the name of the drug and the name of the service user. You must check:

- the service user's name
- the name of the drug
- the dosage
- the frequency of dosage.

Before you administer any medication, ensure that all of these details are correct.

In many workplaces drugs are only administered by a qualified medical practitioner (usually a nurse). In this case, you may still need to assist in the administration. The qualified practitioner will be the person who has the keys to a locked drugs cabinet if any class A drugs (diamorphine, any opiate or barbiturate drugs) are being administered.

As a matter of good practice you should learn about any medication that you are administering to a service user. The rules and regulations which govern qualified medical practitioners such as nurses and midwives require them to understand the nature and potential side effects of any drug they administer. It could be dangerous to hand out medications that you do not understand and whose potential side effects you are unsure of. This could mean you miss the importance of symptoms reported by a service user who has suffered an adverse reaction to a particular medication.

You must also carefully read the instructions on any medication before applying it. This is particularly important if you are using creams, eye or ear drops, or vaginal or anal pessaries. You must ensure that you follow the administration procedures required for the particular drug and report any difficulties in using the drug or administering it.

Refusal or inability to take medication

If a service user is unable to take medication, perhaps because of difficulty in swallowing or because he or she is feeling ill, or is unwilling to take the medication prescribed, then you must immediately report this to your supervisor or line manager, or to the clinical practitioner responsible for prescribing or administering the medicine. You should never allow a situation to continue in the hope that the service user may feel like taking medication later. It is essential to report a missed dose immediately.

Individual medication

All medication is prescribed for a specific individual. When any drug is prescribed, a wide range of factors are taken into account. These include:

▶ other conditions which the service user may have
▶ the service user's age
▶ the service user's size
▶ the social circumstances
▶ the service user's likely ability to take it
▶ any potential side effects, and ability to deal with them.

This range of considerations means that under no circumstances can medication prescribed for one individual be used for another, without the express agreement of a qualified medical practitioner. If you are faced with a situation where service users are sharing medication, you should explain carefully the reasons why medication may have been selected for one individual and why it may be inappropriate for another individual. Tell service users the possible consequences, such as:

▶ an adverse reaction
▶ that the drug will be ineffective
▶ that the drug may react with other medication that is being taken
▶ that it may be at the wrong dosage or concentration
▶ that it may not be in the most appropriate form for that individual to take.

Storage of medicines

All medicines, whether they are potentially dangerous drugs or not, should be stored in a locked cupboard or cabinet. All medicines must be clearly labelled and should be regularly checked for their expiry date. Medicines which are out of date can either become ineffective or can have increased toxicity levels, and thus cause serious problems if they are used after the specified date.

Your workplace will have a system for recording all use of drugs and medications.

Keeping records

Your workplace will have a system for recording the administration and use of any drugs and medications. You should ensure that you complete the necessary documentation and record the administration of any drugs or medicines in the service user's case notes or care plan.

Problems or queries

If a service user has questions, you should answer them within the limits of your knowledge. If you are asked a question about medication which is beyond your knowledge, you must refer the question to a qualified practitioner or to your supervisor. If a service user refuses to take prescribed medication this must be reported immediately to your supervisor and recorded in the case notes or care plan.

Check it out

Check out the procedures for administering medication in your work setting. Find out what the procedures are when a service user refuses medication or if there is evidence that medication is being shared. You should be able to identify from the procedures in your workplace those clinical practitioners who are registered and qualified to prescribe and administer different types of drugs.

Health and fitness for you and your service users

One of the best ways of avoiding accident or injury at work is to keep yourself as fit and healthy as possible – and exactly the same applies for the service users you look after. The healthier and fitter people are, the better the quality of life they can enjoy.

Working in care is a demanding job and you cannot afford to take risks with your own health. Some simple rules will provide you with a basic plan for maintaining a healthy lifestyle. One of the key ways to achieve health and fitness is to eat a healthy diet.

Healthy eating

There are five main food groups. If we eat a variety of foods from these five groups in the proportions recommended by health professionals, we can be

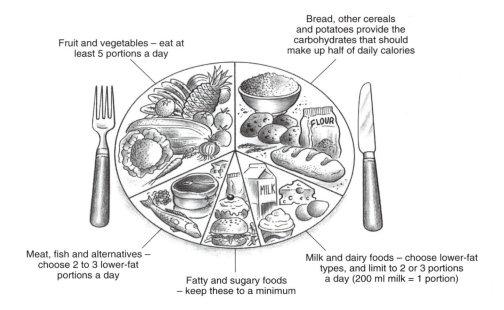

Fruit and vegetables – eat at least 5 portions a day

Bread, other cereals and potatoes provide the carbohydrates that should make up half of daily calories

FLOUR

MILK

Meat, fish and alternatives – choose 2 to 3 lower-fat portions a day

Fatty and sugary foods – keep these to a minimum

Milk and dairy foods – choose lower-fat types, and limit to 2 or 3 portions a day (200 ml milk = 1 portion)

confident of having a nutritionally balanced diet – one that contains all the nutrients we need to stay healthy.

Although water isn't a nutrient, our bodies need it for a number of reasons. We need it to produce sweat which helps control body temperature, to get rid of waste material (in urine and faeces) and for the blood and other body fluids. We should aim to drink at least two pints of water a day.

Food group	Proportion of daily diet	Examples of foods
Bread, other cereals and potatoes	We should aim for this food group to make up about one-third of what we eat every day.	Bread, chapattis, rice, pasta, breakfast cereals, maize, millet, green bananas, potatoes, beans, lentils.
Fruit and vegetables	We should aim for this food group to make up about one-third of what we eat every day. We should try to eat five portions of fruit and vegetables every day.	Fresh, frozen and canned fruit and vegetables.
Meat, fish and alternatives	We should aim for this food group to make up about one-sixth of what we eat every day.	All types of meat (preferably low fat) and fish; eggs, beans, nuts, soya.
Milk and dairy foods	We should aim for this food group to make up about one-sixth of what we eat every day.	Milk, cheese, yoghurt (preferably low fat).

| Foods containing fat and foods containing sugar. | These foods should be eaten only occasionally and in small amounts. | Butter, margarine, mayonnaise, oily salad dressings, crisps, sweetened drinks, ketchup, sweets, biscuits, cakes, puddings. |

The proportions suggested here are only guidelines, because the amount of nutrients that individuals need varies depending on factors such as their age, lifestyle and occupation. For example, someone who leads a very active lifestyle will need more energy-giving foods than someone who has a deskbound job and takes little exercise; and a growing child will need more body-building nutrients than an elderly person.

Check it out

Think about your typical daily diet. Bearing in mind your age, level of activity and job, decide whether you are eating a balanced diet and make a note of how you could change what you eat to ensure that it is balanced.

Also check your fluid intake (not counting coffee and alcohol!). Are you drinking enough water?

Activity and exercise

Many people who work in care have plenty of physical activity at work – some days it feels as if you have walked miles and lifted Olympic weights! However, the human body thrives on physical exercise, and any activity which makes your heart and lungs work harder is good for you. While increasing your activity levels can mean doing something new to you, it can also mean doing just what you usually do but in a more energetic way. Run upstairs instead of walking, or walk upstairs instead of taking the lift! Walk to the shops instead of taking the bus or car. Dancing, swimming, cycling, playing tennis and attending low-impact aerobics classes all offer a relatively painless way of increasing your levels of activity. Activities like these can be great fun when they involve a group of friends, and they are a marvellous way to meet new people and to relax.

Strange as it may seem, the more active you become, the more energy you will seem to have! People who are physically active on a regular basis say that they:

▶ have more energy
▶ have more stamina or staying power
▶ are stronger and leaner (more toned)
▶ have an improved posture, shape and appearance
▶ have more self-confidence and feel better about themselves

- feel more relaxed and rested in general
- sleep better.

Health professionals report that people who are more active have a lower risk of:

- circulatory and heart disease
- respiratory problems
- high blood pressure
- stroke
- osteoporosis (brittle bone disease)
- mental health problems.

Check it out

Do you think that you could benefit from increasing your level of physical activity? If so, make a list of activities you could do.

Rest and sleep

One of the benefits of exercise is that it promotes rest and sleep, which are very important for everyone. When we are resting or asleep:

- our muscles relax
- our blood pressure, pulse rate and body temperature fall
- our digestive system becomes more active so that our meals can be properly digested and our body tissues can become topped up with nutrients.

If we are deprived of rest and sleep, we can

- suffer memory loss
- become irritable and depressed
- lose our ability to think straight and carry out daily tasks.

Check it out

How do you sleep? Well? Or do you find it difficult to get off to sleep or to stay asleep? Keep a record of how you sleep over a period of about a week. Can you see a link between how well you sleep and the types of activities you do when you are awake?

Sleeping is not the only way of resting and relaxing. Rest your body and your mind by:

- switching off from work with a good book or film
- relaxing with friends
- walking or taking other gentle exercise
- playing sport
- just sitting and daydreaming.

These are useful ways of renewing the mental energy as well as the physical energy you need to do your job well.

Check it out

Write a plan for yourself for a typical (and health-conscious) day, which:

- describes what you will eat and drink, and explains your choices
- describes the physical activity you will do
- describes what you will do for relaxation and explains why you choose to relax in this way
- describes how and when you will rest (including sleep) and explains why you need to rest.

Health promotion

Depending on your employer, there may be an in-house health promotion or occupational health unit linked to your workplace. Most NHS hospital or community trusts will have a Health Promotion Unit, and there are national Health Promotion Agencies or Boards for England, Wales, Scotland and Northern Ireland where you can obtain information and advice about maintaining a healthy lifestyle for you, your family and those you care for.

Outcome activity 3.2

This task should be carried out on your own. When you have completed the activity, share your results in a group.

Step 1

Prepare a suitable diary/journal for a working week. Use a computer if possible; you may choose to use the diary/calendar program or to record it in a word-processed document, or even as a spreadsheet. For each day's entry you will need two columns; one headed 'Task' and one headed 'Health and Safety'.

Step 2

Keep a record over a week of all the activities you undertake at work. Make sure you include everything you do – the following may help to remind you of the tasks you do in a day:

> making tea, changing beds, moving a service user from a chair, brushing someone's hair, helping with washing or bathing, helping with toileting, preparing food, helping to serve meals, clearing plates

Include at least 12 different tasks – if you have not done 12 different tasks in a particular week, include some that you know you will do at other times. Put your list of tasks in the first column headed 'Task'.

Step 3

In the second column, record the health and safety issues that you have to take into account for each task. For example, if you were moving someone, you may record 'check lifting equipment'; for bathing, 'check non-slip mat'. You should record as many different health and safety checks as possible for each task.

Step 4

If you are using a computer, e-mail your diary/journal to the other members of your group. If this is not possible, print out and show your work to others so that everyone has a chance to read the diaries. Hold a group discussion about all the different tasks and health and safety issues you have identified. If there are any disagreements, use the Internet or textbooks to research the correct procedures.

This outcome is about first aid, and helping you to understand the actions you should take if a health emergency arises. This is not a substitute for a first aid course, and will give you only an outline of the steps you need to take. You cannot become qualified to deal with these emergencies by studying a book. Unless you have been trained on a first aid course, you should be careful about what you do, because the wrong action can cause more harm to a casualty. It is always best to summon help.

What you can safely do

Most people have a useful role to play in a health emergency, even if it is not dealing directly with the ill or injured person. It is also vital that someone:

- summons help as quickly as possible
- offers assistance to the competent person who is dealing with the emergency
- clears the immediate environment and makes it safe – for example, if someone has fallen through a glass door, the glass must be removed as soon as possible before there are any more injuries
- offers help and support to other people who have witnessed the illness or injury and may have been upset by it. Clearly this can only be dealt with once the ill or injured person is being helped.

REMEMBER

Only attempt what you know you can safely do. Do not attempt something you are not sure of. You could do further damage to the ill or injured person and you could lay yourself and your employer open to being sued. Do not try to do something outside your responsibility or capability – summon help and wait for it to arrive.

How you can help the casualty in a health emergency

It is important that you are aware of the initial steps to take when dealing with the commonest health emergencies. You may be involved with any of these emergencies when you are at work, whether you work in a residential, hospital or community setting. Clearly, there are major differences between the different work situations.

- If you are working in a hospital where skilled assistance is always immediately available, the likelihood of your having to act in an emergency, other than to summon help, is remote.

- In a residential setting, help is likely to be readily available, although it may not necessarily be the professional medical expertise of a hospital.
- In the community you may have to summon help and take action to support a casualty until the help arrives. It is in this setting that you are most likely to need some knowledge of how to respond to a health emergency.

This section gives a guide to recognising and taking initial action in a number of health emergencies:

- severe bleeding
- cardiac arrest
- shock
- loss of consciousness
- epileptic seizure
- choking and difficulty with breathing
- fractures and suspected fractures
- burns and scalds
- poisoning
- electrical injuries.

Severe bleeding

Severe bleeding can be the result of a fall or injury. The most common causes of severe cuts are glass, as the result of a fall into a window or glass door, or knives from accidents in the kitchen.

Symptoms

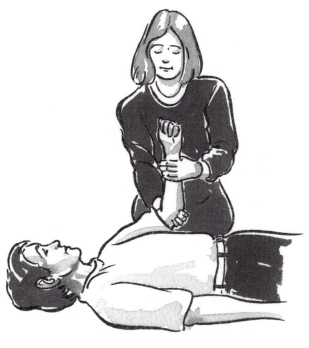

There will be apparently large quantities of blood from the wound. In some very serious cases, the blood may be pumping out. Even small amounts of blood can be very frightening, both for you and the casualty. Remember that a small amount of blood goes a long way, and things may look worse than they are. However, severe bleeding requires urgent medical attention in hospital. Although people rarely bleed to death, extensive bleeding can cause shock and loss of consciousness.

Aims

- To bring the bleeding under control
- To limit the possibility of infection
- To arrange urgent medical attention

Lay the casualty down and raise the affected part.

Action

1 You will need to apply pressure to a wound that is bleeding. If possible, use a sterile dressing. If one is not readily available, use any absorbent material, or even your hand. Do not forget the precautions (see 'Protect yourself' below). You will need to apply direct pressure over the wound for 10 minutes (this can seem like a very long time) to allow the blood to clot.
2 If there is any object in the wound, such as a piece of glass, *do not* try to remove it. Simply apply pressure to the sides of the wound.
3 Lay the casualty down and raise the affected part if possible.
4 Make the person comfortable and secure.
5 Dial 999 for an ambulance.

Protect yourself

You should take steps to protect yourself when you are dealing with casualties who are bleeding. Your skin provides an excellent barrier to infections, but you must take care if you have any broken skin such as a cut, graze or sore. Seek medical advice if blood comes into contact with your mouth, nose or gets into your eyes. Blood-borne viruses (such as HIV or hepatitis) can be passed only if the blood of someone who is already infected comes into contact with broken skin.

▶ If possible, wear disposable gloves.
▶ If possible, wash your hands thoroughly in soap and water before and after treatment.
▶ If this is not possible, cover any areas of broken skin with a waterproof dressing.
▶ Take care with any needles or broken glass in the area.
▶ Use a mask for mouth-to-mouth resuscitation if the casualty's nose or mouth is bleeding.

Cardiac arrest

Cardiac arrest occurs when a person's heart stops. Cardiac arrest can happen for various reasons, the most common of which is a heart attack, but a person's heart can also stop as a result of shock, electric shock, a convulsion or other illness or injury.

Symptoms

▶ No pulse
▶ No breathing

Aims

▶ To obtain medical help as a matter of urgency
▶ It is important to give oxygen, using mouth-to-mouth resuscitation, and to

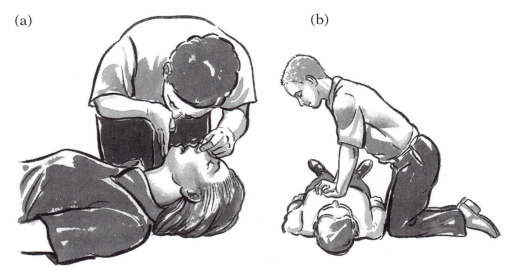

(a)   (b)

Mouth-to-mouth resuscitation (a) and chest compressions (b).

stimulate the heart, using chest compressions. This procedure is called cardio-pulmonary resuscitation – CPR. You will need to attend a first aid course to learn how to resuscitate – you cannot learn how to do this from a book. On the first aid course you will be able to practise on a special dummy.

Action

1 Check whether the person has a pulse and whether he or she is breathing.
2 If not, call for urgent help from the emergency services.
3 Start methods of resuscitation *if* you have been taught how to do it.
4 Keep up resuscitation until help arrives.

Shock

Shock occurs because blood is not being pumped around the body efficiently. This can be the result of loss of body fluids through bleeding, burns, severe vomiting or diarrhoea, or a sudden drop in blood pressure or a heart attack.

Symptoms

The signs of shock are easily recognised. The person:

▶ will look very pale, almost grey
▶ will be very sweaty, and the skin will be cold and clammy
▶ will have a very fast pulse
▶ may feel sick and may vomit
▶ may be breathing very quickly.

Aims

▶ To obtain medical help as a matter of urgency
▶ To improve blood supply to heart, lungs and brain

Raise the feet off the ground and keep the casualty warm.

Action

1 Call for urgent medical assistance.
2 Lay the person down on the floor. Try to raise the feet off the ground to help the blood supply to the important organs.
3 Loosen any tight clothing.
4 Watch the person carefully. Check the pulse and breathing regularly.
5 Keep the person warm and comfortable, but *do not* warm the casualty with direct heat, such as a hot water bottle.

Do not:

▶ allow casualty to eat or drink
▶ leave the casualty alone, unless it is essential to do so briefly in order to summon help.

Loss of consciousness

Loss of consciousness can happen for many reasons, from a straightforward faint to unconsciousness following a serious injury or illness.

Symptom

A reduced level of response and awareness. This can range from being vague and 'woozy' to total unconsciousness.

Aims

▶ To summon expert medical help as a matter of urgency
▶ To keep the airway open
▶ To note any information which may help to establish the cause of the unconsciousness

Action

1 Make sure that the person is breathing and has a clear airway.
2 Maintain the airway by lifting the chin and tilting the head backwards.

Open the airway.

3 Look for any obvious reasons why the person may be unconscious, such as a wound or an ID band telling you of any condition he or she has. For example, many people who have medical conditions which may cause unconsciousness, such as epilepsy or diabetes, will wear special bracelets or necklaces giving information about their condition.

4 Place the casualty in the recovery position (see below), *but not if you suspect a back or neck injury*, until the emergency services arrive.

Do not:

▶ attempt to give anything by mouth
▶ attempt to make the casualty sit or stand
▶ leave the casualty alone, unless it is essential to leave briefly in order to summon help.

The recovery position

Many of the actions you need to take to deal with health emergencies will involve you in placing someone in the recovery position. In this position a casualty has the best chance of keeping a clear airway, not inhaling vomit and remaining as safe as possible until help arrives. This position should *not* be attempted if you think someone has back or neck injuries, and it may not be possible if there are fractures of limbs.

(a)

(b)

(c)

The recovery position.

1 Kneel at one side of the casualty, at about waist level.

2 Tilt back the person's head – this opens the airway. With the casualty on his or her back, make sure that limbs are straight.

3 Bend the casualty's near arm as if waving (so it is at right angles to the body). Pull the arm on the far side over the chest and place the back of the hand against the opposite cheek (**a** in diagram opposite).

4 Use your other hand to roll the casualty towards you by pulling on the far leg, just above the knee (**b** in the diagram). The casualty should now be on his or her side.

5 Once the casualty is rolled over, bend the leg at right angles to the body. Make sure the head is tilted well back to keep the airway open (**c** in diagram).

Epileptic seizure

Epilepsy is a medical condition that causes disturbances in the brain which result in sufferers becoming unconscious and having involuntary contractions of their muscles. This contraction of the muscles produces the fit or seizure. People who suffer with epilepsy do not have any control over their seizures, and may do themselves harm by falling when they have a seizure.

Aims

▶ To ensure that the person is safe and does not injure himself or herself during the fit
▶ To offer any help needed following the fit

Action

1 Try to make sure that the area in which the person has fallen is safe.
2 Loosen all clothing.
3 Make sure that the person is comfortable and safe. Particularly try to prevent head injury.
4 Once the seizure has ended, make sure that the person has a clear airway and place in the recovery position.
5 If the fit lasts longer than five minutes, or you are unaware that the casualty is a known epileptic, call an ambulance.

Do not:

▶ attempt to hold the casualty down, or put anything in the mouth
▶ move the casualty until he or she is fully conscious, unless there is a risk of injury in the place where he or she has fallen.

Choking and difficulty with breathing (in adults and children over 8 years)

This is caused by something (usually a piece of food) stuck at the back of the throat. It is a situation which needs to be dealt with, as people can quickly stop breathing if the obstruction is not removed.

Symptoms

▶ Red, congested face at first, later turning grey
▶ Unable to speak or breathe, may gasp and indicate throat or neck

Aims

▶ To remove obstruction as quickly as possible
▶ To summon medical assistance as a matter of urgency if the obstruction cannot be removed

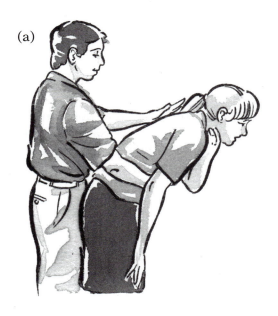

Dealing with an adult who is choking.

Action

1 Try to get the person to cough. If that is not immediately effective, move on to step 2.
2 Bend the person forwards. Slap sharply on the back between the shoulder blades up to five times (**a** in diagram above).
3 If this fails, stand behind the person with your arms around him or her. Join your hands just below the breastbone. One hand should be in a fist and the other holding it (**b** in the diagram).
4 Sharply pull your joined hands upwards and into the person's body at the same time. The force should expel the obstruction.
5 You should alternate backslaps and abdominal thrusts until you clear the obstruction.

Fractures and suspected fractures

Fractures are breaks or cracks in bones. They are usually caused by a fall or other type of injury. The casualty will need to go to a hospital as soon as possible to have a fracture diagnosed correctly.

Symptoms

▶ Acute pain around the site of the injury
▶ Swelling and discoloration around the affected area
▶ Limbs or joints may be in odd positions
▶ Broken bones may protrude through the skin

Action

1 The important thing is to support the affected part. Help the casualty to find the most comfortable position.
2 Support the injured limb in that position with as much padding as necessary – towels, cushions or clothing will do.
3 Take the person to hospital or call an ambulance.

Do not:

▶ try to bandage or splint the injury
▶ allow the casualty to have anything to eat or drink.

Support the injured limb.

Burns and scalds

There are several different types of burn; the most usual are burns caused by heat or flame. Scalds are caused by hot liquids. People can be burned by chemicals or by electrical currents.

Symptoms

▶ Depending on the type and severity of the burn, skin may be red, swollen and tender, blistered and raw or charred
▶ Usually severe pain and possibly shock

Aims

▶ To obtain immediate medical assistance if the burn is over a large area (as big as the casualty's hand or more) or is deep
▶ To send for an ambulance if the burn is severe or extensive. If the burn or scald is over a smaller area, the casualty could be transported to hospital by car
▶ To stop the burning and reduce pain
▶ To minimise possibility of infection

Action

1 For major burns, summon immediate medical assistance.
2 Cool down the burn. Keep it flooded with cold water for 10 minutes. If it is a chemical burn, this needs to be done for 20 minutes.

Cool the burn with water.

Ensure that the contaminated water used to cool a chemical burn is disposed of safely.

3 Remove any jewellery, watches or clothing which are not sticking to the burn.

4 Cover the burn if possible, unless it is a facial burn, with a sterile or, at least, clean dressing. For a burn on a hand or foot, a clean plastic bag will protect it from infection until it can be treated by an expert.

If clothing is on fire, remember the basics: *stop*, *drop*, *wrap* and *roll* the person on the ground.

Do not:

▶ remove anything which is stuck to a burn
▶ touch a burn, or use any ointment or cream
▶ cover facial burns – keep pouring water on until help arrives.

REMEMBER

If a person's clothing is on fire, STOP – DROP – WRAP – ROLL:

▶ *Stop* him or her from running around.
▶ *Get* him/her to *drop* to the ground – push him/her if you have to and can do so safely.
▶ *Wrap* him/her in something to smother the flames – a blanket or coat, anything to hand. This is better if it is soaked in water.
▶ *Roll* him/her on the ground to put out the flames.

Poisoning

People can be poisoned by many substances, drugs, plants, chemicals, fumes or alcohol.

Symptoms

Symptoms will vary depending on the poison.

▶ The person could be unconscious
▶ There may be acute abdominal pain
▶ There may be blistering of the mouth and lips.

Aims

▶ To remove the casualty to a safe area if he/she is at risk, and it is safe for you to move him/her
▶ To summon medical assistance as a matter of urgency

- To gather any information which will identify the poison
- To maintain a clear airway and breathing until help arrives

Action

1 If the casualty is unconscious, place him/her in the recovery position to ensure that the airway is clear, and that he/she cannot choke on any vomit.
2 Dial 999 for an ambulance.
3 Try to establish what the poison is and how much has been taken. This information could be vital in saving a life.
4 If a conscious casualty has burned mouth or lips, he or she can be given small frequent sips of water or cold milk.

Do not try to make the casualty vomit.

Electrical injuries

Electrocution occurs when an electrical current passes though the body.

Symptoms

Electrocution can cause cardiac arrest and burns where the electrical current entered and left the body.

Aims

- To remove the casualty from the current when you can safely do so
- To obtain medical assistance as a matter of urgency
- To maintain a clear airway and breathing until help arrives
- To treat any burns

Action

There are different procedures to follow depending on whether the injury has been caused by a high or low voltage current.

Injury caused by high voltage current

This type of injury may be caused by overhead power cables or rail lines, for example.

1 Contact the emergency services immediately.
2 *Do not* touch the person until all electricity has been cut off.
3 If the person is unconscious, clear the airway.
4 Treat any other injuries present, such as burns.
5 Place in the recovery position until help arrives.

Injury caused by low voltage current

This type of injury may be caused by powered kettles, computers, drills, lawnmowers, etc.

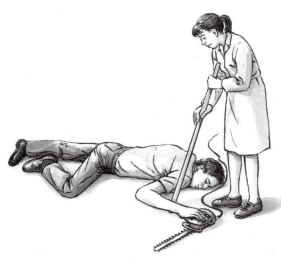

Move the casualty away from the current.

1 Break the contact with the current by switching off the electricity at the mains if possible.

2 It is vital to break the contact as soon as possible, *but* if you touch a person who is 'live' (still in contact with the current) you too will be injured. If you are unable to switch off the electricity, then you must stand on something dry which can insulate you, such as a telephone directory, rubber mat or a pile of newspapers, and then move the casualty away from the current as described below.

3 Do not use anything made of metal, or anything wet, to move the casualty from the current. Try to move him/her with a wooden pole or broom-handle, even a chair.

4 Alternatively, drag him/her with a rope or cord or, as a last resort, pull by holding any of the person's dry clothing which is *not* in contact with his/her body.

5 Once the person is no longer in contact with the current, you should follow the same steps as with a high voltage injury.

Check it out

1 You should always attempt first aid even if you have not been trained, because it is always better to do something. True or false?

2 What is the single most important act for an untrained person to do in a health emergency?

Other ways to help

Summon assistance

In the majority of cases this will mean telephoning 999 and requesting an ambulance. It will depend on the setting in which you work and clearly is not required if you work in a hospital! But it may mean calling for a colleague with medical qualifications, who will then be able to make an assessment of the need for further assistance. Similarly, if you work in the residential sector, there should be a medically qualified colleague available. If you are the first on the scene at an emergency in the community, you may need to summon an ambulance for urgent assistance.

If you need to call an ambulance, try to keep calm and give clearly all the details you are asked for. Do not attempt to give details until they are asked for – this wastes time. Emergency service operators are trained to find out the necessary information, so let them ask the questions, then answer calmly and clearly.

Follow the action steps outlined in the previous section while you are waiting for help to arrive.

Assist the person dealing with the emergency

A second pair of hands is invaluable when dealing with an emergency. If you are assisting someone with first aid or medical expertise, follow all his or her instructions, even if you don't understand why. An emergency situation is not the time for a discussion or debate – that can happen later. You may be needed to help to move a casualty, or to fetch water, blankets or dressings, or to reassure and comfort the casualty during treatment.

Make the area safe

An accident or injury may have occurred in an unsafe area – and it was probably for precisely that reason that the accident occurred there! Sometimes, it may be that the accident has made the area unsafe for others. For example, if someone has tripped over an electric flex, there may be exposed wires or a damaged electric socket. Alternatively, a fall against a window or glass door may have left shards of broken glass in the area, or there may be blood or other body fluids on the floor. You may need to make the area safe by turning off the power, clearing broken glass or dealing with a spillage.

It may be necessary to redirect people away from the area of the accident in order to avoid further casualties.

Maintain the privacy of the casualty

You may need to act to provide some privacy for the casualty by asking onlookers to move away or stand back. If you can erect a temporary screen with coats or blankets, this may help to offer some privacy. It may not matter to the casualty at the time, but he or she has a right to privacy if possible.

Make accurate reports

You may be responsible for making a report on an emergency situation you have witnessed, or for filling in records later. Concentrate on the most important aspects of the incident and record the actions of yourself and others in an accurate, legible and complete manner. See the example of an accident report on page 104.

How to deal with witnesses' distress – and your own

People who have witnessed accidents can often be very distressed by what they have seen. The distress may be as a result of the nature of the injury, or the

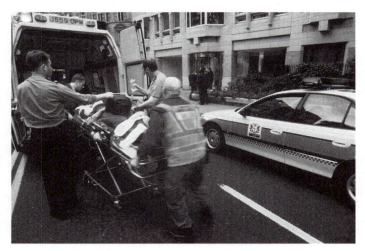

Witnessing accidents is often distressing.

blood loss. It could be because the casualty is a friend or relative or simply because seeing accidents or injuries is traumatic. Some people can become upset because they feel helpless and do not know how to assist, or they may have been afraid and then feel guilty later.

You will need to reassure people about the casualty and the fact that he or she is being cared for appropriately. However, do not give false reassurance about things you may not be sure of.

You may need to allow individuals to talk about what they saw. One of the commonest effects of witnessing a trauma is that people need to repeat over and over again what they saw.

What about you?

You may feel very distressed by the experience you have gone through. You may find that you need to talk about what has happened, and that you need to look again at the role you played. You may feel that you could have done more, or you may feel angry with yourself for not having a greater knowledge about what to do.

There is a whole range of emotions which you may experience. You should be able to discuss your feelings with your supervisor and use any support provided by your employer.

If you have followed the basic guidelines in this outcome, you will have done as much as could be expected of anyone at the scene of an emergency who is not a trained first aider.

Outcome activity 3.3

You could undertake this activity in a group or by yourself. You are to produce an explanatory report, which can be completed as a word-processed document in hard copy or viewed on-line.

Step 1
Read the following scenario:

You are a support worker in the community and are visiting an older service user, Mrs J. She lives alone, but has friends and relatives who also visit. You go twice each week to provide general support services.

When you arrive one day, you are met with the following scene. Mrs J is lying on the floor, looking grey, and is cold and clammy. Her breathing is very shallow and infrequent, and she does not appear to be conscious. Her sister, Mrs P, who was visiting when she was taken ill, tried to help her and fell against the fireplace, badly cutting her leg which is bleeding heavily. She is conscious, but in a lot of pain. An elderly neighbour, Mrs N, heard the crash and commotion and is also there. She does not appear to be hurt, but is very pale and trembling.

Step 2
Explain what actions you would take, and in what order. Use bullet points, or a numbered list, or a table. Make sure that you explain why you would take each of the actions listed, and give reasons for the order in which you would do them.

Protect people from abuse

In this unit you will look at some of the most difficult issues that you will face as a care professional. For many people, starting work in care means coming to terms with the fact that some service users will be subjected to abuse by those who are supposed to care for them. For others it will not be the first time that they have been close to an abuse situation, either through personal experience or previous professional involvement.

Regardless of previous experience, coming face to face with situations where abuse is, or has been, taking place is difficult and emotionally demanding. Knowing what you are looking for, and how to recognise it, is an important part of ensuring that you are making the best possible contribution to protecting service users from abuse. You need to know how society handles abuse, how to recognise it, and what to do about it. It is a tragic fact that almost all disclosures of abuse are true – and you will have to learn to *think the unthinkable*.

The forms of abuse which you will need to be aware of and to understand are abuses which are suffered by service users at the hands of someone who is providing care for them – abusers can be parents, informal carers, care professionals and/or the policies and practices of the care setting itself. This outcome is not about abuse by strangers, which needs to be dealt with in the same way as any other crime.

If you can learn always to consider the possibility of abuse, always to be alert to potentially abusive situations and always to *listen* and *believe* when you are told of abuse, then you will provide the best possible protection for the service users you care for. Taking the right steps when faced with an abusive situation is the second part of your key contribution to service users who are, or have been, abused.

Outcome 1: Identify the signs of abuse and appropriate strategies to respond to it

Forms of abuse

Abuse can take many forms. These are usually classified under five main headings:

▶ physical
▶ sexual

- emotional
- financial
- institutional.

Abuse can happen to any service user regardless of his or her age or service needs. Child abuse is the most well-known and well-recognised type of abuse, but all service user groups can suffer abuse. Abuse of the elderly and of those with learning difficulties, sensory impairment or physical disabilities is just as common, but often less well recognised.

Physical abuse

Any abuse involving the use of force is classified as physical abuse. This can mean:

- punching, hitting, slapping, pinching, kicking, in fact any form of physical attack
- burning or scalding
- restraint such as tying people up or tying them to beds or furniture
- refusal to allow access to toilet facilities
- deliberate starvation or force feeding
- leaving service users in wet or soiled clothing or bedding as a deliberate act, to demonstrate the power and strength of the abuser
- excessive or inappropriate use of medication
- a carer causing illness or injury to someone he or she cares for in order to gain attention (this is called 'Munchausen's syndrome by proxy').

Sexual abuse

Sexual abuse, whether of adults or children, is also abuse of a position of power. Children can never be considered to give informed consent to any sexual activity of any description. For many adults, informed consent is not possible because of a limited understanding of the issues. In the case of other adults, consent may not be given and the sexual activity is either forced on the individual against his or her will or the individual is tricked or bribed into it.

Sexual activity is abusive when informed consent is not freely given. It is important to recognise the difference between the freely consenting sexual activity of adults who also happen to be service users, and those situations where abuse is taking place because of the powerful position of someone who is supposed to be providing care.

Sexual abuse can consist of:

- sexual penetration of any part of the body with a penis, finger or any object
- touching inappropriate parts of the body or any other form of sexual contact without the informed agreement of the service user

- sexual exploitation
- exposure to, or involvement in, pornographic or erotic material
- exposure to, or involvement in, sexual rituals
- making sexually related comments or references which provide sexual gratification for the abuser
- making threats about sexual activities.

Emotional abuse

All the other forms of abuse have an element of emotional abuse. Any situation which means that a service user becomes a victim of abuse at the hands of someone he or she trusted is, inevitably, going to cause emotional distress. However, some abuse is purely emotional – there are no physical, sexual or financial elements involved. This abuse can take the form of:

- humiliation, belittling, putting down
- withdrawing or refusing affection
- bullying
- making threats
- shouting, swearing
- making insulting or abusive remarks
- racial abuse
- constant teasing and poking fun.

Financial abuse

Many service users are very vulnerable to financial abuse, particularly those who may have a limited understanding of money matters. Financial abuse, like all other forms of abuse, can be inflicted by professional or informal carers and can take a range of forms, such as:

- stealing money or property
- allowing or encouraging others to steal money or property
- tricking or threatening service users into giving away money or property
- persuading service users to take financial decisions which are not in their interests
- withholding money, or refusing access to money
- refusing to allow service users to manage their own financial affairs
- failing to support service users in managing their own financial affairs.

Institutional abuse

Institutional abuse is not only confined to the large-scale physical or sexual abuse scandals of the type which are regularly publicised in the media. Of course this type of systematic and organised abuse goes on in residential and hospital settings, and must be recognised and dealt with appropriately so that service users can be protected. However, service users can be abused in many other ways in settings where they could expect to be cared for and protected. For example:

▶ service users in residential settings are not given choice over day-to-day decisions such as mealtimes, bedtimes, etc.
▶ freedom to go out is limited by the institution
▶ privacy and dignity are not respected
▶ personal correspondence is opened by staff
▶ the setting is run for the convenience of staff, not service users
▶ excessive or inappropriate sedation/medication are given
▶ access to advice and advocacy is restricted or not allowed
▶ complaints procedures are deliberately made unavailable.

You can probably begin to see that the different types of abuse are often interlinked, and service users can be victims of more than one type of abuse. Abuse is a deliberate act – it is something which someone actively does in order to demonstrate power and authority over another person. It is also done with the motive of getting some sort of gratification for the abuser.

Check it out

How many types of abuse does your workplace have guidelines to deal with? Look at the policy and procedures for dealing with abuse. See how many types of abuse are listed and what the procedures are. If you cannot find any information, ask your supervisor.

Neglect

Neglect is very different from abuse. Whereas abuse involves a deliberate act, neglect happens when care is not given and a service user suffers as a result. The whole area of neglect has many aspects which you need to take into account, but there are broadly two different types of neglect:

▶ self-neglect
▶ neglect by others.

Self-neglect

Many people neglect themselves; this can be for a range of reasons. People may be ill or depressed and unable to make the effort, or not feel capable of looking after themselves. Sometimes people feel that looking after themselves is unimportant. Others may choose to live in a different way that does not match up to the expectations of other people. Working out when someone is neglecting himself or herself, given all of these considerations, can be very difficult.

Self-neglect can show itself in a range of ways:

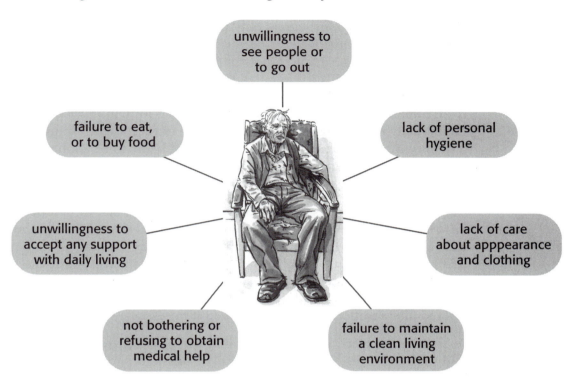

However, what may appear to be self-neglect may, in fact, be an informed choice made by someone who does not regard personal and domestic cleanliness or hygiene as priorities. It is always important to make a professional judgement based on talking with the service user and finding out his or her wishes, before making any assumptions about what may be needed.

Neglect by others

This occurs when either a professional or informal carer is caring for a service user and the care needs of the service user are not met. Neglect can happen because those responsible for providing the care do not realise its importance, or because they cannot be bothered, or choose not, to provide it. As the result of neglect, service users can become ill, hungry, cold, dirty, injured or deprived of their rights. Neglecting someone you are supposed to be caring for can mean failing to undertake a range of care services, for example:

▶ not providing adequate food
▶ not providing assistance with eating food if necessary
▶ not ensuring that the service user receives personal care

- ▶ not ensuring that the service user is adequately clothed
- ▶ leaving the service user alone
- ▶ failing to maintain a clean and hygienic living environment
- ▶ failing to obtain necessary medical/health-care support
- ▶ not supporting social contacts
- ▶ not taking steps to provide a safe and secure environment for the service user.

In some care situations, carers may fail to provide some aspects of care because they have not been trained, or because they work in a setting where the emphasis is on cost saving rather than care provision. In these circumstances it becomes a form of institutional abuse. Unfortunately, there have been residential care homes and NHS trusts where service users have been found to be suffering from malnutrition as the result of such neglect. Individual workers who are deliberately neglecting service users in spite of receiving training and working in a quality caring environment are, fortunately, likely to be spotted very quickly by colleagues and supervisors.

However, carers who are supporting service users in their own homes are in different circumstances, often facing huge pressures and difficulties. Some may be reluctantly caring for a relative because they feel they have no choice; others may be barely coping with their own lives and may find caring for someone else a burden they are unable to bear. Regardless of the many possible reasons for the difficulties which can result in neglect, it is essential that a suspicion of neglect is investigated and that concerns are followed up so that help can be offered and additional support provided if necessary.

As with self-neglect, it is important that lifestyle decisions made by service users and their carers are respected, and full discussions should take place with service users and carers where there are concerns about possible neglect.

Signs and symptoms which may indicate abuse

One of the most difficult aspects of dealing with abuse is to admit that it is happening. If you are someone who has never come across deliberate abuse before, it is hard to understand and to believe that it is happening. It is not the first thing you think of when a service user has an injury or displays a change in behaviour. However, you will need to accept that abuse does happen, and is relatively common. Considering abuse should be the first option when a service user has an unexplained injury or a change in behaviour which has no obvious cause.

Abuse happens to children and adults. Victims often fail to report abuse for a range of reasons:

- ▶ they are too ill, frail or too young
- ▶ they do not have enough understanding of what is happening to them
- ▶ they are ashamed and believe that it is their own fault
- ▶ they have been threatened by the abuser or are afraid
- ▶ they do not think that they will be believed
- ▶ they do not believe that anyone has the power to stop the abuse.

Given the fact that relatively few victims report abuse without support, it is essential that those who are working in care settings are alert to the possibility of abuse and are able to recognise possible signs and symptoms. Signs and symptoms can be different in adults and children and you need to be aware of both, because regardless of the setting you work in you will come into contact with both adults and children. Your responsibilities do not end with the service user group you work with. If you believe that you have spotted signs of abuse of anyone, you have a duty to take the appropriate action.

Information on signs and symptoms comes with a warning – none of the signs or symptoms is always the result of abuse, and not all abuse produces these signs and symptoms. They are a general indicator that abuse should be considered as an explanation. You and your colleagues will need to use other skills, such as observation and communication with other professionals, in order to build up a complete picture.

Signs of possible abuse in adults

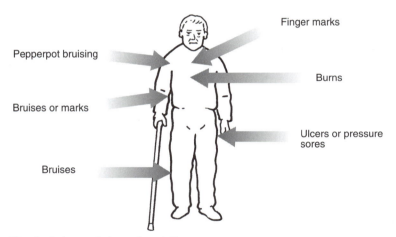

Finger marks

Pepperpot bruising

Burns

Bruises or marks

Ulcers or pressure sores

Bruises

Physical signs of abuse in adults.

Abuse can often show as physical effects and symptoms. These are likely to be accompanied by emotional signs and changes in behaviour, but this is not always the case.

Any behaviour changes could indicate that the service user is a victim of some form of abuse, but remember that they are only an indicator and will need to be linked to other factors to arrive at a complete picture.

Type of sign/ symptom	Description of sign/symptom	Possible form of abuse indicated
Physical	frequent or regular falls or injuries	physical
Physical	'pepperpot bruising' – small bruises, usually on the chest, caused by poking with a finger or pulling clothes tightly	physical
Physical	fingermarks – often on arms or shoulders	physical
Physical	bruising in areas not normally bruised, such as the insides of thighs and arms	physical
Physical	unusual sexual behaviour	sexual
Physical	blood or marks on underclothes	sexual
Physical	recurring genital/urinary infections	sexual

Type of sign/symptom	Description of sign/symptom	Possible form of abuse indicated
Physical	marks on wrists, upper arms or legs which could be from tying to a bed or furniture	physical/sexual
Physical	burns or scalds in unusual areas such as soles of feet, insides of thighs	physical
Physical	ulcers, bedsores or rashes caused by wet bedding/clothing	physical
Physical	missing cash or belongings, or bank accounts with unexplained withdrawals	financial
Physical	missing bank account records	financial
Emotional/behavioural	becoming withdrawn or anxious	all forms of abuse
Emotional/behavioural	loss of interest in appearance	sexual/physical/emotional
Emotional/behavioural	loss of confidence	sexual/physical/emotional
Emotional/behavioural	sudden change in attitude to financial matters	financial
Emotional/behavioural	becoming afraid of making decisions	emotional
Emotional/behavioural	sleeping problems	all forms of abuse
Emotional/behavioural	changes in eating habits	all forms of abuse
Emotional/behavioural	no longer laughing or joking	all forms of abuse
Emotional/behavioural	feeling depressed or hopeless	all forms of abuse
Emotional/behavioural	flinching or appearing afraid of close contact	physical
Emotional/behavioural	unusual sexual behaviour	sexual

Signs of possible abuse in children

This is not a comprehensive list of every indicator of abuse. It is not possible to be exhaustive, neither does the existence of one of these signs mean that abuse

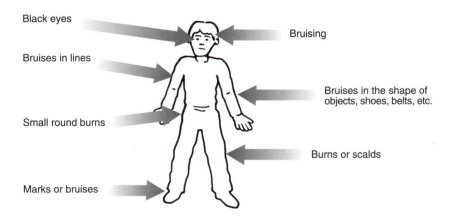

Black eyes

Bruising

Bruises in lines

Bruises in the shape of
objects, shoes, belts, etc.

Small round burns

Burns or scalds

Marks or bruises

Physical signs of abuse in children.

has definitely taken place. Each is an *indicator* which needs to used alongside your other skills, such as observation and listening. It is a further piece of evidence – often the conclusive one – in building a complete picture.

Type of sign/ symptom	Description of sign/symptom	Possible form of abuse indicated
Physical	bruising, or injuries which the child cannot explain	physical
Physical	bruises in the shape of objects – belt buckles, soles of shoes, etc.	physical
Physical	handmarks	physical
Physical	bruises in lines	physical
Physical	injuries to the frenulum (the piece of skin below the tongue), or between the upper and lower lips and the gums	physical
Physical	black eyes	physical
Physical	bruising to ears	physical
Physical	burns, particularly small round burns which could have come from a cigarette	physical
Physical	burns in lines, like the elements of an electric fire	physical
Physical	burns or scalds to buttocks and backs of legs	physical
Physical	complaints of soreness or infections in the genital/anal area	sexual
Physical	frequent complaints of abdominal pain	sexual

Type of sign/ symptom	Description of sign/symptom	Possible form of abuse indicated
Physical	deterioration of personal hygiene	sexual/neglect
Emotional/ behavioural	sudden change in behaviour, becoming quiet and withdrawn	sexual/emotional
Emotional/ behavioural	change to overtly sexual behaviour, or an obsession with sexual comments	sexual
Emotional/ behavioural	problems sleeping or onset of nightmares	sexual/emotional
Emotional/ behavioural	a sudden unwillingness to change clothes or participate in sports	sexual/physical
Emotional/ behavioural	finding excuses not to go home	physical/sexual/ emotional
Emotional/ behavioural	appearing tense or frightened with a particular adult	physical/sexual/ emotional

Check it out

Ask one of your experienced colleagues, or your supervisor, if he or she can recall a situation where abuse was suspected. Ask about the signs and symptoms that caused concern, and the steps that were taken to investigate them.

Carer behaviour which should alert you to possible abuse

Sometimes, it is not the behaviour of the service user which is the first noticeable feature of an abusive situation. It can be that the first behaviour you notice is that of the carer. The following are some indications of behaviour which may give cause for concern, although with the usual warning that each is only a possible indicator of problems:

▶ reluctance to allow visitors to see the service user
▶ insistence on being present with service user at all times
▶ derogatory or angry references to the service user
▶ excessive interest in financial accounts or assets
▶ excessive requests for repeat prescriptions.

Who can abuse?

Abuse can take place at home or in a formal care setting. At home, it could be an informal carer who is the abuser, although it could be a neighbour or regular visitor. It can also be a professional care worker who is carrying out the abuse. This situation can mean that abuse goes undetected for some time because of the unsupervised nature of a carer's visits to someone's home.

In a formal care setting, abuse may be more likely to be noticed, although some of the more subtle forms of abuse, such as humiliation, can sometimes be so commonplace that they are not recognised as abusive behaviour.

Abuse is not only carried out by individuals; groups, or even organisations, can also create abusive situations. It has been known that groups of carers in residential settings can abuse individuals in their care. Often people will act in a different way in a group than they would alone. Think about teenage 'gangs', which exist because people are prepared to do things jointly which they would not think to do if they were by themselves.

No dear, you can't go out now, you nearly slipped last time. You can't go on your own and I don't have anyone to send with you – can't you see how busy we all are?

Abuse in a care setting may not just be at the hands of members of staff. There is also abuse which comes about because of the way in which an establishment is run, where the basis for planning the systems, rules and regulations is not the welfare, rights and dignity of the residents or patients, but the convenience of the staff and management. This is the sort of situation where people can be told when to get up and go to bed, given communal clothing, only allowed medical attention at set times and not allowed to go out. This is referred to as 'institutional abuse'.

REMEMBER

Abusers can be:

▶ individuals
▶ groups
▶ organisations.

Julie was 43, and she had worked as a senior support worker in a residential unit for people with a learning disability for the past five years. Julie loved her job and was very committed to the residents in the unit. She was very concerned for the welfare of the people she supported and did everything she could for them. Many of them had been in the unit for many years and Julie knew them well. The unit was not very large and had only a small staff who were able to work very closely with the resident group.

Julie and the other staff were concerned that the residents could easily be taken advantage of, as some were not able to make effective judgments about other people and potentially risky situations.

Regular mealtimes were arranged so that everyone could share the day's experiences and talk together, and bedtimes and getting-up times were also strictly adhered to. The staff found that this was a good way of keeping the residents organised and motivated. Residents did not go out into the local town in the evenings because of the potential safety risk, but the staff would plan evenings of TV watching, choosing programmes which they thought would interest the residents. Sometimes simple games sessions or walks in the local park were arranged.

A new manager was appointed to the unit and Julie and the other staff were very surprised to find that the new manager was horrified by many of these practices, and wanted to make major changes.

1 What changes do you think the manager may have suggested?
2 Why do you think those changes may be needed?
3 Do you consider that Julie and the other staff members were practising in the best way for the residents?
4 Think about, or discuss, whether this situation was abusive.

Up to this point, consideration has been given to abuse by carers, whether parents, informal or professional. But do not forget that in residential or hospital settings, abuse can occur between residents or patients, and it can also happen between visitors and residents or patients. People can also abuse themselves.

Self-harm

The one abuser it is very hard to protect someone from is himself or herself. Individuals who self-harm will be identified in their plan of care, and responses to their behaviour will be recorded. You must ensure that you follow the agreed plan for provision of care for someone who has a history of self-harm. It is usual that an individual who is at risk of harming himself or herself will be closely supported and you may need to contribute towards activities or therapies which have been planned for the individual.

Why does abuse happen?

One of the key contributions you can make towards limiting abuse is to be aware of where abuse may be happening. It is not easy to accept that abuse is going on, and it is often simpler to find other explanations.

Be prepared to *think the unthinkable*. If you know about the circumstances in which abuse has been found to occur most frequently, then you are better able to respond quickly if you suspect a problem.

It is not possible accurately to predict situations where abuse will take place – a great deal of misery could be saved if it were. It is possible, though, to identify some factors which seem to make it more likely that abuse could occur. This does not mean that abuse will definitely happen – neither should you assume that all people in these circumstances are potential abusers – but it does mean that you should be aware of the possibility when you are dealing with these situations.

Situations when vulnerable adults may be abused at home

Adults may be abused at home in situations where:

▶ carers have had to change their lifestyles unwillingly
▶ the dependent person has communication problems, has had a personality or behaviour change (such as dementia), rejects help or is aggressive
▶ there is no support from family or professional carers
▶ carers are becoming dependent on drugs or alcohol
▶ carers have no privacy
▶ the dependent person is difficult and inconsiderate.

Situations when child abuse can happen

Child abuse can happen in situations where:

▶ parents are unable to put a child's needs first
▶ parents or carers feel a need to show dominance over others
▶ parents or carers have been poorly parented themselves
▶ parents or carers were abused themselves as children
▶ families have financial problems (this does not just mean families on low incomes)
▶ families have a history of poor relationships or of use of violence.

Check it out

Think about the service users you deal with. Make a list of how many of them fit into the circumstances outlined. Now resolve to keep a particular eye on those service users and watch for any signs that abuse may be happening. Be prepared to *think the unthinkable*.

Situations when abuse can happen in a care setting

Abuse can happen in a care setting when:

▶ staff are poorly trained or untrained
▶ there is little or no management supervision or support
▶ staff work in isolation
▶ there are inadequate numbers of staff to cope with the workload
▶ there are inadequate security arrangements
▶ there is no key worker system and good relationships are not formed between staff and residents.

Check it out

Look at your workplace. Do any of the above points apply? If any of these are the case in your workplace, you need to be aware that people can be put under so much stress that they behave abusively. Remember that abuse is not just about physical cruelty.

If none of these things happen in your workplace, then try to imagine what work would be like if they did. Sit down with a colleague, if you can, and discuss what you think the effects of any two of the items in the list would be. If you cannot do this with a colleague, you can do it on your own by making notes.

If you want to be effective in helping to stop abuse you will need to:

▶ believe that abuse happens
▶ recognise abusive behaviour

There are many factors involved in building protection against abuse.

▶ be aware of when abuse can happen
▶ understand who abusers can be
▶ know the policies and procedures for handling abuse
▶ follow the individual's plan of care
▶ recognise likely abusive situations
▶ report any concerns or suspicions.

Your most important contribution will be to be *alert*. For example, an individual's plan of care or your organisational policy should specify ways in which the individual's whereabouts are constantly monitored – and if you are alert to where a vulnerable person is, and who he or she is with, you can do much to help avoid abusive situations.

The effects of abuse

Abuse devastates those who suffer it. It causes people to lose their self-esteem and their confidence. Many adults and children become withdrawn and difficult to communicate with. Anger is a common emotion among people who have been abused. It may be directed against the abuser, or at those people around them who failed to recognise the abuse and stop it happening.

One of the greatest tragedies is when people who have been abused turn their anger against themselves and blame themselves for everything that has happened to them. These are situations which require expert help, and this should be available to anyone who has been abused, regardless of the circumstances.

In an earlier section of this outcome you learned about the signs and symptoms of abuse. Some of the behaviour changes which can be signs of abuse can become permanent, or certainly very long-lasting. There are very few survivors of abuse whose personality remains unchanged, and for those who do conquer the effects of abuse, it is a long, hard fight.

The abuser, often called the 'perpetrator', also requires expert help, and this should be available through various agencies depending on the type and seriousness of the abuse. People who abuse, whether their victims are children or vulnerable adults, receive very little sympathy or understanding from society. There is no public recognition that some abusers may have been under tremendous strain and pressure, and abusers may find that they have no support from friends or family. Many abusers will face the consequences of their actions alone.

DID YOU KNOW?

Prisoners who are serving sentences for child abuse, or for abuse of vulnerable adults, have to be kept in separate areas of the prison for their own safety. If they were allowed to mix with other prisoners, they could be seriously assaulted or even killed.

Care workers who have to deal with abusive situations will have different emotional reactions. There is no 'right way' to react. Everyone is different and will deal with things in his or her own way. If you have to deal with abuse, these are some of the ways you may feel, and some steps you can take which may help.

Shock

You may feel quite traumatised by the abusive incident. It is quite normal to find that you cannot get the incident off your mind, that you have difficulty concentrating on other things, or that you keep having 'flashbacks' and re-enact the situation in your head. You may also feel that you need to keep talking about what happened.

Talking can be very beneficial, but if you are discussing an incident outside your workplace, you must remember rules of confidentiality and *never* use names. You will find that you can talk about the circumstances just as well by referring to 'the boy' or 'the father' or 'the daughter'. This way of talking does become second nature, and is useful because it allows you to share your feelings about things which have happened at work while maintaining confidentiality.

These feelings are likely to last for a fairly short time, and are a natural reaction to shock and trauma. If at any time you feel that you are having difficulty, you must talk to your manager or supervisor, who should be able to help.

Anger

Alternatively, the situation may have made you feel very angry, and you may have an overwhelming urge to inflict some damage on the perpetrator of the abuse. While this is understandable, it is not professional and you will have to find other ways of dealing with your anger. Again, your supervisor or manager should help you to work through your feelings.

Everyone has different ways of dealing with anger, such as taking physical exercise, doing housework, punching a cushion, writing feelings down and then tearing the paper up, crying or telling your best friend. Whatever you do with your anger in ordinary situations, you should do the same in this situation (just remember to respect confidentiality if you need to tell your best friend – miss out the names). It is perfectly legitimate to be angry, but you cannot bring this anger into the professional relationship.

Distress

The situation may have made you distressed, and you may want to go home and have a good cry, or give your own relatives an extra hug. This is a perfectly normal reaction. No matter how many years you work, or how many times it happens, you may still feel the same way.

Some workplaces will have arrangements in place where workers are able to share difficult situations and get support from each other. Others may not have any formal meetings or groups arranged, but colleagues will offer each other support and advice in an informal way. You may find that work colleagues who have had similar experiences are the best people with whom to share your feelings.

There is, of course, the possibility that the situation may have brought back painful memories for you of abuse you have suffered in your own past. This is often the most difficult situation to deal with, because you may feel as if you should be able to help because you know how it feels to be abused, but your own experience has left you without any room to deal with the feelings of others. There are many avenues of support now available to survivors of abuse. You can find out about the nearest support confidentially, if you do not want your workplace colleagues or supervisor to know.

There is no doubt that dealing with abuse is one of the most stressful aspects of working in care. There is nothing odd or abnormal about feeling that you need to share what you have experienced and looking for support from others. This is a perfectly reasonable reaction and, in fact, most experienced managers would be far more concerned about a worker involved in dealing with abuse who appears quite unaffected by it, than about one who comes looking for guidance and reassurance.

REMEMBER

▶ Feeling upset is normal.

▶ Talk about the incident if that helps, but respect the rules of confidentiality and miss out the names.

▶ Being angry is OK, but deal with it sensibly – take physical exercise, do the housework, cry.

▶ Do not be unprofessional with the abuser.

▶ If you are a survivor of abuse and you find it hard to deal with, ask for help.

How the law affects what you do

Much of the work in caring is governed by legislation, but the only group where legislation specifically provides for protection from abuse is children. Older people, people with a learning disability, physical disabilities or mental health problems have service provision, restrictions, rights and all sorts of other requirements laid down in law, but no overall legal framework to provide protection from abuse. The laws which cover your work in the field of care are summarised in the table on page 150.

There are, however a number of sets of guidelines, policies and procedures in respect of abuse for service user groups other than children, and you will need to ensure that you are familiar with policies for your area of work and particularly with those policies which apply in your own workplace.

Service user group	Laws which govern their care	Protection from abuse?
Children	Children Act 1989	Yes
People with mental health problems	Mental Health Act 1983	No
Adults with a learning disability	Mental Health Act 1983	No
Adults with disabilities	Chronically Sick and Disabled Persons Act 1986 Disability Discrimination Act 1995	No
Older people	National Assistance Act 1948 NHS and Community Care Act 1990	No
All service user groups	Care Standards Act 2000	Yes, through raising standards

Check it out

Ask your supervisor if there are any laws or guidelines which govern the procedures in your workplace for dealing with abuse. There should be a written policy and guidelines to be followed if abuse is suspected.

Recent policy approaches to protecting children and vulnerable adults have concentrated on improving and monitoring the quality of the service provided to them. The principle behind this is that if the overall quality of practice in care is constantly improved, then well-trained staff working to high standards are less likely to abuse service users, and are more likely to identify and deal effectively with any abuse they find.

Government policies and guidelines for children

The most important set of government guidelines which lays down practices for co-operation between agencies is called 'Working Together to Safeguard Children'. It was published in 1999 and forms the basis for present child protection work. This guideline ensures that information is shared between agencies and professionals, and that decisions in respect of children are not taken by just one person.

The government produced a Green Paper called 'Every Child Matters' in late 2003. Among other changes, this paper proposes that co-operation between agencies is no longer sufficient to protect children, and that local authorities must appoint a Director for Children's Services, to replace the present directors of social services and of education. It is hoped that bringing the two departments together in this way will improve the services for children, and encourage better communication and ways of working together.

What about vulnerable adults?

The government has published a set of guidelines about adults, called 'No Secrets'. These guidelines state that older people have specific rights, which include being treated with respect, and being able to live in their home and community without fear of physical or emotional violence or harassment.

The guidance gives local authorities the lead responsibility in co-ordinating the procedures. Each local authority area must have a management committee for the protection of vulnerable adults, which will develop policies, protocols and practices. The guidance covers:

▶ identification of those at risk
▶ setting up a framework for different agencies to co-operate
▶ developing procedures for responding in individual cases
▶ recruitment, training and other staff and management issues.

Vulnerable adults are entitled to respect and the full protection of the law.

A government White Paper published in 2001, 'Valuing People: A New Strategy for Learning Disability in the 21st Century', sets out the ways in which services for people with a learning disability will be improved. 'Valuing People' sets out four main principles for providing services for people with a learning disability:

▶ civil rights
▶ independence
▶ choice
▶ inclusion.

The White Paper also makes it clear that people with a learning disability are entitled to the full protection of the law.

What does the law say about protecting children?

The Children Act 1989 requires that local authority social services departments provide protection from abuse for children in their area. The Act of Parliament gives powers to social services departments, following the procedures laid down by the Area Child Protection Committee, to take legal steps to ensure the safety of children. Following the consultation on the Green Paper 'Every Child Matters' (see above), the procedures and bodies concerned will change and new legislation will be developed.

What happens in an emergency?

The three agencies able to take legal steps to protect children.

In an emergency, at the moment, a social worker or an NSPCC officer can apply to a magistrate for an order to look after a child. This is an Emergency Protection Order (known as an EPO). The police are also able to take immediate steps to protect children in an emergency situation. (This is a Police Protection Order, or PPO.) These orders require evidence which shows that there is reasonable cause to believe that a child may suffer 'significant harm'. They are short-term orders, usually for 3–7 days, and are followed by a court hearing where more detailed evidence is produced and the parents are represented.

Not all investigations into abuse are emergencies, and not all involve legal proceedings. Some abusive, or potentially abusive, situations are dealt with by working with the family, usually by agreeing a 'contract' between social services and the family.

What does the law say about protecting vulnerable adults?

The Acts of Parliament which are mainly concerned with provisions for vulnerable adults are the National Assistance Act 1948 and the NHS and Community Care Act 1990. They do not specifically give social services departments a 'duty to protect' but, of course, people are protected by the law. If a vulnerable adult is abused and that abuse is considered to be a criminal offence, then the police will act. It is sometimes thought that if the victim is confused, a prosecution will not be brought – this is not so. All vulnerable adults will have the full protection of the law if any criminal offences are committed.

Some vulnerable adults suffer abuse in residential or hospital settings. These settings are controlled by legislation. Hospitals have complaints procedures and arrangements for allowing 'whistle-blowers' who have concerns about abuse to come forward. Residential homes and nursing homes have to be registered with the National Care Standards Commissioner, who will investigate allegations of abuse and can ultimately close an unsatisfactory residential home or nursing home.

The Mental Health Act 1983 (and the draft Mental Health Bill) forms the framework for service provision for people with mental health problems and people with a learning disability. There are provisions within this legislation for social services departments to assume responsibility for people who are so 'mentally impaired' that they are not able to be responsible for their own affairs. This is called **guardianship**. However, like all other vulnerable adults, there is no specific duty to protect people from abuse.

The government White Paper published in 2001, 'Valuing People' (see page 151) will form the basis for services to all people with a learning disability and will provide rights, but no specific duty of protection.

The Chronically Sick and Disabled Persons Act and the Disability Discrimination Act provide disabled people with rights, services and protection from discrimination, but they do not provide any means of comprehensive protection from abuse.

As with all vulnerable groups, there is a long and tragic history to the physical and emotional abuse suffered by people with physical disabilities or a learning disability. Public humiliation and abuse of those with mental health problems is still visible today, so it is hardly surprising that abuse on an individual level is still all too commonplace.

What happens in an emergency?

Many social services departments now have procedures in place similar to those for protecting children. There will be an investigation of the alleged or suspected abuse, followed by a case conference where information will be shared between all the professionals concerned and a plan of action will be worked out. The vulnerable adult concerned and/or a friend or advocate will also be invited to take part in the conference if he or she wishes.

What if a professional carer abuses?

There are special procedures in place for investigating abuse which is inflicted by care workers or foster carers. It is investigated by an outside agency and immediate steps are taken to remove the suspected abuser (often called the 'perpetrator') from contact until the investigation has been completed.

These issues are well publicised at the moment, as many cases of systematic and long-term abuse by care workers are coming to light.

How to share information

Sharing information between different agencies and organisations can often be a vital way of ensuring that people at risk are protected.

There are often several care and other professionals involved with any child or adult considered to be at risk. One of the most important features of work with people at risk is co-operation between agencies.

Teamwork is vital, both with other involved professional care workers and within your own team. Information is always clearer and more comprehensive when it is shared, and you may find that different members of the team have observed slightly different aspects and so the picture will become more complete.

It may also be possible that people will have different views on any allegations or incidents which have taken place. It is important that all these views are taken into account. Some of the professionals involved may be working with the person alleged to be the abuser and they may have a different perspective to add to any discussions. Remember that there is always more than one story to be told, even though it may not always be easy to take account of the alleged abuser's perspective.

DID YOU KNOW?

Every report (called a Fatal Case Inquiry) into child deaths from abuse in the past 30 years has highlighted the need for agencies to co-operate, work together and share information.

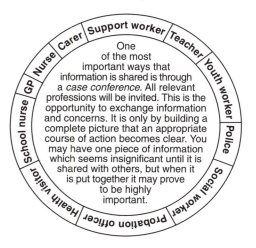

One of the most important ways that information is shared is through a *case conference*. All relevant professions will be invited. This is the opportunity to exchange information and concerns. It is only by building a complete picture that an appropriate course of action becomes clear. You may have one piece of information which seems insignificant until it is shared with others, but when it is put together it may prove to be highly important.

Sharing information.

Each local area, at the moment, has an Area Child Protection Committee (ACPC), which includes representatives of all relevant professionals: social workers, health professionals, teachers, police, and so on. The ACPC meets to lay down procedures which must be followed where child abuse is suspected or confirmed. It also ensures that a register of children who have been abused, or are at risk of abuse, is maintained by the social services department.

The Child Protection Register is a record of all the children about whom there are concerns. The register is held and maintained by social services, but the information can be shared with other relevant professionals. There are four main categories in the register: physical abuse, sexual abuse, neglect and emotional abuse.

Although there is no legal requirement for such a register for vulnerable adults, local authorities could make this part of the policy they develop as a result of the 'No Secrets' guidelines (see page 151).

DID YOU KNOW?

Anyone, including a child, who has been abused by someone who has been tried in court and found guilty, can receive Criminal Injuries compensation. It is also possible for cases to be brought even where there is no criminal trial. It is vital that anyone who has been abused in any way should have a solicitor to act in his or her interests.

Ways of assessing risk

Decisions about abuse of adults are different from those about children because, ultimately, it is the adult himself or herself who will make the decision about how to proceed. Clearly there are some situations where this is not possible, but such circumstances are provided for under the law. If an adult has been abused, but he or she decides to remain in the abusive situation, then there are generally no legal steps which can be taken to prevent that.

CASE STUDY

Mrs C is 75 years old. She is quite fit, although increasingly her arthritis is slowing her down and making her less steady on her feet. She has been a widow for 15 years and lives with her only son, R, who is 51. When R was 29, he was involved in a motorcycle accident which caused brain damage, from which he has never fully recovered. His speech is slow and he sometimes has problems in communication. His co-ordination and fine motor skills have been affected, so he has problems with buttons, shoelaces and writing. R also suffers from major mood swings and can be aggressive. Mrs C is R's only carer. He has never worked since the accident, but he goes to a day centre three days each week. Mrs C takes the opportunity to go to a day centre herself on those three days because she enjoys the company, the outings and activities.

Recently, Mrs C has had an increasing number of injuries. In the past two months she has had a grazed forehead, a black eye, a split lip and last week she arrived at the day centre with a bruised and sprained wrist. She finally admitted to the centre staff that R had inflicted the injuries during his periods of bad temper. She said that these were becoming more frequent as he became more frustrated with her slowness.

Despite being very distressed, Mrs C would not agree to being separated from R. She was adamant that he didn't mean to hurt her. She would not consider making a complaint to the police. Finally, Mrs C agreed to increasing both her and R's attendance at their day centres, and to having some assistance with daily living.

1 What do you think Mrs C should have done?
2 Can she be left with R?
3 Why do you think Mrs C will not take any action against R?

This kind of situation may cause a great deal of concern and anxiety for the care workers, but there are limits on the legal powers to intervene and there is no justification for removing Mrs C's right to make her own decisions.

Care workers faced with an abusive situation which cannot be resolved must assess the risks and work out ways of minimising the likelihood of further abuse. A **risk assessment** will be carried out. Your workplace will have procedures about the way in which a risk assessment is carried out and how decisions are made. Many workplaces will have a system where decisions about the level of risk are taken by a case conference. In others, decisions may be made by a team manager, who would need to know all the available facts. At no time would any worker be expected to make such judgements and decisions alone, or to accept full responsibility for this type of assessment.

DID YOU KNOW?

This type of shared responsibility and decision-making has developed only over the past 30 years or so in the case of children, and far more recently in the case of adults. Before that, workers were often left to make decisions without any support, and took the full weight of blame if things went wrong.

A risk assessment will consider all the elements in a situation and try to reach a judgement about potential dangers and what can be done. Clearly, the options are far more limited in respect of adults, because there is no overall legislation offering protection. It is also very rarely possible to act against the will of an adult, even where it may be in his or her best interests.

What to do if you suspect abuse in your own workplace

Blowing the whistle

One of the most difficult situations to deal with is when you believe that abuse is happening in your workplace. It is often hard to accept that the people you work with would abuse, but if you have evidence or good grounds for concern, then you will have to take action.

- The first step is to report the abuse to your manager.
- If you suspect that your manager is involved, or will not take action, you must refer it to the most senior manager who is likely to be impartial.
- If you do not believe that it is possible to report the abuse to anyone within your workplace, you should contact social services (or the NSPCC, if you prefer, for children).
- If you work for the NSPCC, social services or the health service and you are concerned about abuse, you should still follow the same steps, although you may need to contact a senior manager who is not directly involved with your workplace.

If you do not believe that there is anyone within your workplace or organisation who would take action on any concerns, or if you have reported concerns and nothing has been done, you should contact the National Care Standards Commission, which is responsible for registering and inspecting all health and care services. The Commission will investigate your concerns.

Outcome activity 4.1

You can complete this activity by yourself, or in a group. The task is to produce an information pack which can be used by all members of staff who have to deal with a situation involving abuse. You should assume that all staff will have access to a computer, so if you prefer, you can produce an on-line information pack.

Step 1
Make a list of all the different forms of abuse and neglect. Include a brief explanation of each form you identify.

Step 2
Make a list of the kinds of behaviour changes which may indicate that abuse has taken place. Show which type of abuse may be indicated by the behaviour changes.

Step 3
Describe the policies and procedures of the organisation you work for which are designed to protect service users from abuse. Make notes about how these fit in with legal requirements.

Step 4
Research national and local sources of support for people who have been abused. Include in your pack information about the services offered, who can use them, contact points, addresses, websites and details of the type of support which can be provided.

Behaviour which is unacceptable

All abusive behaviour is unacceptable. However, you may come across other kinds of behaviour which you may not be able to define directly as abusive, but which are close to it – or could lead to an abusive situation if not dealt with.

Generally, you can define behaviour as unacceptable if:

- ▶ it is outside what you would normally see in that situation
- ▶ it does not take into account the needs or views of others
- ▶ people are afraid or intimidated
- ▶ people are undermined or made to feel guilty
- ▶ the behaviour is likely to cause distress or unhappiness to others.

Examples of unacceptable behaviour include:

- ▶ threatening violence
- ▶ subjecting someone to unwelcome sexual attention
- ▶ shouting or playing loud music in a quiet area, or late at night
- ▶ verbal abuse, racist or sexist taunts
- ▶ spreading malicious gossip about someone
- ▶ attempting to isolate someone.

All of these types of behaviour are oppressive to others and need to be challenged. You can probably think of many other situations in your own workplace which have caused unhappiness. You may have had to deal with difficult situations, or have seen others deal with them, or perhaps you have wished that you had done something to challenge unacceptable behaviour.

Unacceptable behaviour from colleagues

You may come across unacceptable and oppressive behaviour in your colleagues or other professionals in your workplace. Behaviour which is abusive is dealt with in the first outcome of this unit. But you may see or hear a colleague behaving in a way which, while it is not abusive as such, may be oppressive and unacceptable. This can take various forms, such as:

- ▶ speaking about service users in a derogatory way
- ▶ speaking to service users in a rude or dismissive way
- ▶ humiliating service users
- ▶ undermining people's self-esteem and confidence
- ▶ bullying or intimidation
- ▶ patronising and talking down to people
- ▶ removing people's right to exercise choice

- failing to recognise and treat people as individuals
- not respecting people's culture, values and beliefs.

In short, the types of behaviour which are unacceptable from workers in care settings are those which simply fail to meet the standards required of good quality practitioners. Any care worker who fails to remember that all people are individuals and all have a right to be valued and accepted, is likely to fall into oppressive or inappropriate behaviour.

Check it out

Ask three colleagues in your workplace to state one behaviour that they would find unacceptable in (a) a service user and (b) a colleague. Compare the six answers and see if they have anything in common. Find out from your supervisor about the type of behaviour that is challenged in your workplace, and that which is allowed.

How to challenge unacceptable behaviour

Steps in dealing with difficult situations

Step 1 Consider all the people involved in the situation

If you have some knowledge of an individual's background, culture and beliefs, it may be easier to see why he or she is behaving in a particular way. This does not make it acceptable, just easier to understand. For example, an individual who has been in a position of wealth or power may be used to giving people instructions and expecting to have immediate attention, and may be quite rude if it does not happen. People may also become aggressive or disruptive because they:

- are frustrated about having to submit to rules of behaviour, and feel their choices are restricted
- feel they have been ignored, insulted or their rights have been denied
- are suffering ill-health, or the side-effects of medication
- have learned in the past that this behaviour will gain them attention or other benefits
- have taken alcohol or illicit drugs.

None of these reasons means that aggression is going to be tolerated, but approaching the situation with some understanding allows people to maintain their dignity while adapting their behaviour.

Step 2 Be aware of everyone's needs

If you are in a work situation, it can be complicated by the fact that the person whose oppressive behaviour you are challenging may also be one of your service users. In this case, it is important to ensure that you challenge the behaviour without becoming aggressive or intimidating yourself, and that you do not undermine the individual.

Step 3 Decide on the best approach

How you decide to deal with an incident of unacceptable behaviour will depend on:

▶ whether the behaviour is violent or non-violent – if the behaviour is violent, what the potential dangers of the situation are, who may be in danger and what needs to be done to help those in danger
▶ who is involved, and how well you know them and know how to deal with them
▶ whether you need help, and who is available to help you
▶ whether the cause is obvious and the solution is easy to find.

Clearly, you will need to weigh up the situation quickly, in order to deal with it promptly. You will, no doubt, feel under pressure, as this is a stressful situation to be in, whether you are experienced or not. Try to remain calm and think clearly.

Step 4 Deal with non-violent behaviour

If the behaviour you have to deal with is not physical aggression or violence, then you will need to ensure that you challenge it in a situation which provides privacy and dignity. You should challenge without becoming aggressive; remain calm and quietly state what you consider to be unacceptable about the behaviour. Do not try to approach the subject from various angles, or drop hints. Be clear about the problem and what you want to happen.

For example: 'Bill, you have been playing your radio very loudly until quite late each night. Other residents are finding it difficult to get to sleep. I would like you to stop playing it so loudly if you want to have it on late.' You may well have to negotiate with Bill about times, and the provision of headphones, but do not be drawn into an argument and do not be sidetracked into irrelevant discussions. Keep to the point:

Bill: 'Who's been complaining? No one's complained to me. Who is it?'

You: 'Bill, this is about your radio being too loud. The issue is not about who complained, but about the fact that it is upsetting residents and I want you to stop doing it.'

By the end of this discussion, Bill should be very clear about what is being required of him and be in no doubt that his behaviour will have to change.

Unit 4 Protect people from abuse

Step 5 Attempt to calm a potentially violent situation

It is always better to avoid a violent situation than to respond to one, so you need to be aware of the signals which may indicate that violence could erupt. Be on the lookout for verbal aggression; raised volume and pitch of voice; threatening and aggressive gestures; pacing up and down; quick, darting eye movements; prolonged eye contact.

Try to respond in ways least likely to provoke further aggression.

▶ Use listening skills, and appear confident (but not cocky).
▶ Keep your voice calm and at a level pitch.
▶ Do not argue.
▶ Do not get drawn into prolonged eye contact.
▶ Attempt to defuse the situation with empathy and understanding. For example: 'I realise you must be upset if you believe that George said that about you. I can see that you're very angry. Tell me about what happened.'

Be prepared to try a different approach if you find you are not getting anywhere. Always make sure that an aggressor has a way out with dignity, both physically and emotionally.

DID YOU KNOW?

There is a technique which is recommended for use in situations which become violent. It is called 'Breakaway' and is approved by the Home Office for use in all types of care settings. It provides you with methods for dealing with a physical threat or attack without causing injury. Ask your employer to arrange for you to attend a course with an approved trainer.

Check it out

Your workplace should have a policy on dealing with aggression and violence. Ask to see it and make sure that you read it carefully.

How to deal with abusive behaviour

Most of the time, your role in dealing with abuse will be the vital one of being aware of the possibility of abuse, reporting and recording any concerns you have, or reporting any disclosure made to you.

However, there may be occasions when you have to intervene in order to prevent an abusive situation developing. The abuse can be physical, verbal or behavioural. This is most likely to happen in a hospital, residential or day-care setting between patients or service users. If you work in the community, you could be in the situation of having to deal with abusive behaviour from a carer. If you do have to act directly to prevent abuse, you need to take the following steps.

▶ Always prevent a situation if you can. If you know, for example, that two people regularly disagree violently about everything from politics to whether or not it is raining, try to arrange that they are involved in separate activities and, if possible, have seats in separate lounges! Alternatively, you may decide to deal with the situation by talking to them both, and offering to help them resolve their disagreements.

▶ Deal with abusive behaviour in the same way as aggression – be calm and be clear. Do not get drawn into an argument and do not become aggressive, but make it very clear that abusive behaviour will not be tolerated.

▶ Only intervene directly if there is an immediate risk. You will need to use your communication skills to ensure that you handle the situation in a way that does not make things worse and will ensure that you protect the person at risk.

Rules for dealing with abusive behaviour
1 Avoid it if possible.
2 Try to get people talking.
3 Keep calm. Be clear.
4 Be assertive, never aggressive.

▶ If there is not an immediate risk, report the incident and get assistance as soon as possible.

▶ If you do have to intervene in an abusive situation, you will need to behave assertively. Do not shout, panic or get into an argument. State firmly and clearly what you want to happen – 'Mary, stop hitting Enid now!' You can deal with the consequences a little later, but the key action is to stop the abuse – 'Lee, stop calling Mike those names and move away from him now!' There must be no mistake about what has to happen. This is not the time to discuss it, this is the time to stop it – the discussion comes later.

▶ If you have witnessed, or intervened in, an act of abuse which may constitute a criminal offence, you must *not* remove any possible evidence until the police have examined the scene.

Check it out

Ask an experienced colleague if he or she has ever been in the situation of having to act to stop abuse or likely abuse. Ask how your colleague handled the situation. Does he or she think it was handled well, or could it have been dealt with in a better way? Would it have turned out differently?

Once the immediate risk has been averted, you must then report the incident to your manager, and the correct procedures for dealing with abuse must be followed. You are not in a position to take a decision about what is and what is not serious enough to be followed up. That is a decision which will be taken after discussion with the agencies involved.

Where there are injuries, or the possibility of physical evidence, as in sexual abuse, then a medical examination must be carried out. If an adult has been abused, he or she must consent to an examination before one can be carried out. In the case of a child, the parents must consent, unless they are the suspected abusers.

Use of physical restraint

Physically restraining service users is very much a last resort and restraint should be used only if it is absolutely unavoidable. Every workplace has a policy on the use of physical restraint, and you will need to be sure that you know what it is for your own setting. The policies vary, but are likely to include the following principles.

- Before using restraint, staff should have good grounds for believing that immediate action is necessary to prevent a service user from significantly injuring himself/herself or others, or causing serious damage to property.
- Staff should take steps in advance to avoid the need for physical restraint, such as by discussing or providing diversion from the problem; and the service user should be warned that physical restraint will be used unless he or she stops.
- Only the minimum force necessary to prevent injury or damage should be used.
- Every effort should be made to have other staff present before applying restraint. These staff can act both as assistants and witnesses.
- As soon as it is safe, restraint should be gradually relaxed to allow the service user to regain self-control.
- Restraint must be an act of care and control, not punishment.
- Physical restraint must never be used purely to force service users to comply with staff instructions when there is no immediate risk to people or property.

These are the general principles, but you must also act within the law. Excessive use of physical restraint can be viewed as assault, and result in a criminal charge. This is why it is essential that you follow your workplace policy, and discuss with your supervisor exactly what steps you must take. All workplaces are likely to provide training in the use of physical restraint and methods of managing aggression, so make sure that you take up any opportunity to receive training.

Being involved in an incident of violence or aggression can be very distressing and you should ask for support from your supervisor if you find that you are affected by an incident you have witnessed or been involved in.

Recording an incident

It is also important that you write a report of the incident as soon as possible. You may think that you will never forget what you saw or heard, but details do become blurred with time and repetition. Your workplace may have a special form or you may have to write a report. If there is a reason why writing a report is not possible, then you should record your evidence on audio tape. It is not acceptable to pass on the information verbally – there must be a record which can be referred to. Your evidence may be needed by the social workers and police officers who will investigate the situation. It may be useful for a doctor who will conduct an examination, or it may be needed for the case conference or for court proceedings.

Check it out

Think about the children's game of Chinese Whispers. The players sit in a circle and a message is whispered from one person to the next around the circle. The last player speaks the message aloud. It has usually changed quite a lot as it has been passed around the circle!

So it is easy to see how verbal information can become distorted, or messages lose their emphasis, as they are retold. Always make sure you record information as soon as you can.

Minimising the risk of aggression or abuse

No one can guarantee that all aggressive or abusive behaviour can be prevented – human beings have always abused each other in one form or another. However, using the information you have about possible abusive situations, you are now able to work towards preventing abuse by recognising where it can happen. When risk situations occur in the community, you may be in a position to intervene directly or to report to your supervisor and offer suggestions about ways to reduce risks.

Try to ensure that people in potentially abusive situations are offered as much support as possible. A carer, whether of a child or an adult, is less likely to resort to abuse if he or she feels supported, acknowledged and appreciated. Showing sympathy and understanding for a person's situation can often defuse potential explosions. A care worker could express this by saying: 'It must be so hard caring for your mother. The demands she makes are so difficult. I think you are doing a wonderful job.' Such comments can often help a carer to feel that he or she does have someone who understands and has some interest in supporting him or her. So many times the focus is on the individual in need of care, and the carer is ignored.

DID YOU KNOW?

There is a saying that 'The best way to keep on caring *about* someone is not to have to care *for* them'. There are many thousands of carers looking after relatives who would testify to the truth of that saying.

Providing support

Some situations require much more than words of support, and giving practical, physical support to a carer or family may help to reduce the risk of abuse. The extra support provided by a professional carer can do this in two ways: firstly, it can provide the additional help which allows the carer to feel that he or she is not in a hopeless never-ending situation; and secondly, it can provide a regular opportunity to check an individual where abuse is suspected or considered to be a major risk.

There is now legislation protecting carers, and their situation is acknowledged as being very stressful and demanding. The Carers (Recognition and Services) Act 1995 means that carers have the right to ask for an assessment of their own needs. The national strategy for carers, 'Caring about Carers' (1999), identifies funding for support, information and consultation for carers. All of this can contribute to easing the burden on carers, and thus reducing the chances of abuse.

When resources are provided within the community rather than at home, this also offers a chance to observe someone who is thought to be at risk. Day centres, training centres, schools, after-school clubs and youth centres also provide an opportunity for people to talk to staff and to feel that they are in a supportive environment where they can talk about any abuse they have suffered and they will be believed and helped.

REMEMBER

▶ Preventing abuse is better than dealing with it.

▶ Support may make all the difference to a carer under stress.

▶ Only intervene directly if there is an immediate risk.

▶ Act assertively to stop any aggressive or abusive behaviour.

Outcome activity 4.2

In this activity, you will show your knowledge about the ways in which aggression can be dealt with. You can either work alone and write a short story, or work in a group and develop a role play which you then perform. Regardless of which approach you choose, the steps to follow are similar.

Step 1

Think of a situation involving aggression which could take place in any care setting. The situation must involve at least one service user and one staff member; other service users and staff members can be involved as observers or in providing support. The scenario should show how the aggressive behaviour developed, and its main cause. You should also show in detail how the situation built up and how it became clear that the service user was becoming aggressive. Your story or role play must describe how the staff member dealt with the episode, and the results. Do not forget to include information about the effects of the incident on service users and staff who were not directly involved.

Step 2

If you are working alone, word process your short story; if you are in a group, work together to plan the presentation of your role play. Make sure that everyone playing a role understands the feelings of the person he or she is portraying.

Step 3

If you have written a short story, present it to your group, either by reading it aloud or by printing and circulating copies. Lead a discussion about how the main characters in your story felt, and why they reacted in the way they did.

If you have prepared a role play, present it to your group and then hold a discussion, with each participant describing in full the feelings of the person he or she played.

Step 4

Lead your discussion to a conclusion about how effective the approach to the aggressive situation was, and the likely outcomes of different approaches.

Glossary

Advocacy The process of speaking or acting to protect an individual's rights.

Assessment tools Formal methods of collecting information to enable an assessment to be made.

Awareness agencies Agencies supplying information about specific issues or conditions.

Care plan The outline of an individual's present and future needs and how these are to be met.

Care standards Defined standards of good practice which can be measured and evaluated.

Care team Those people who have a responsibility for the care of an individual including the person himself or herself.

Care work The process of supporting people with their personal needs.

Challenging behaviour Behaviour that is demanding and/or disruptive and which results in difficulties in providing quality care.

Client The individual who is receiving care, e.g. service users, residents in residential care, patients in acute settings.

Client-centred approach The client's needs determine the plan of care rather than the services that are available.

COSHH Control of Substances Hazardous to Health.

ESOL English for speakers of other languages.

Experiential learning Learning from experience.

Holistic Consideration of the person as a whole, not just seeing each part/problem in isolation.

Management of continence The means by which individuals can be helped to achieve continence or the practical measures to help them cope with incontinence.

Medipak A labelled container with instructions for clear use of day and time of intake.

Multi-disciplinary approach Different disciplines having an understanding of each other's roles and responsibilities in respect of an individual's care.

Multi-disciplinary team People from different disciplines who work together and have responsibility for a person's care.

Multi-disciplinary work The process of working with other disciplines to provide care for an individual.

National Occupational Standard Standards set and agreed nationally by employers and other interested parties as to what constitutes best practice in particular occupational areas.

Norton pressure system A system for assessing the individual's susceptibility to develop pressure sores.

Personal profile Details of an individual's life, background and experience which enables others to see him or her as a whole person.

PISCES/SPICES Physical, Intellectual, Social, Cultural, Emotional, Spiritual needs, Sexual needs.

Preventative Actions which are designed to stop something undesirable from happening.

Quality standards Standards set locally which are used to gauge the quality of the service provided.

Reflective learning The consideration of action so that skills, knowledge, values and emotional response can be developed.

Reflective practitioner A worker who considers his or her actions so that skills, knowledge, values and emotional response can be developed.

Remedial Putting actions into place which will counteract or remove anything unwanted.

RIDDOR Reporting of Injuries, Diseases and Dangerous Occurrences Regulations

SMART Specific, Measurable, Achievable, Realistic, Targeted/Timed, normally related to objectives.

Target groups The people for whom a specific service is intended.

Therapeutic A structured programme of activities designed specifically to effect some change in an individual's behaviour or condition.

Transactions The way that individuals conduct their relationships.

Key skills

	Communication	Application of number	IT	Improving own learning and performance	Problem solving	Working with others
Outcome Activity 1.1 (page 21)	✓		✓		✓	✓
Outcome Activity 1.2 (page 27)	✓		✓		✓	✓
Outcome Activity 1.3 (page 32)	✓		✓		✓	✓
Outcome Activity 1.4 (page 42)	✓		✓		✓	
Outcome Activity 2.1 (page 67)	✓			✓		✓
Outcome Activity 2.2 (page 73)	✓			✓		✓
Outcome Activity 2.3 (page 79)	✓		✓	✓		✓
Outcome Activity 3.1 (page 91)	✓	✓	✓			
Outcome Activity 3.2 (page 117)	✓		✓			✓
Outcome Activity 3.3 (page 132)	✓		✓		✓	
Outcome Activity 4.1 (page 157)	✓		✓			
Outcome Activity 4.2 (page 166)	✓		✓		✓	✓

Index

Headings in *italics* refer to publications. Page numbers in *italics* refer to illustrations.